RESTORATION IN THE CHURCH

Restoration in the Church

Terry Virgo

Cityhill Publishing
Columbia, Missouri

ISBN 0-939159-14-7

'*I* dedicate this book to the man who calls me his "son in the Lord," deeply grateful that God ever gave me such a wonderful pastor as E.G. Rudman. His personal devotion to the Lord has always inspired me, and his constant faithfulness and encouragement to me when I seem to have turned upside down so many things which he held dear have been a source of great joy.

In his old age he has become a true Simeon. Not content to be only righteous and devout, he is still looking with openness and expectation, pointing the way to others.

ACKNOWLEDGEMENTS

I owe an enormous debt of gratitude to many. My heartfelt thanks go to my friends and colleagues in ministry, who have continually exhorted me to keep writing when other demands seemed to say it was impossible.

I am deeply grateful for all those whose words and lives have helped shape my thinking and clarify my vision. Many a burden expressed in this book has its origin in the inspiration of other servants of God too numerous to name.

I thank God for the church at Clarendon, so faithful in their prayer support.

Pam Haworth, my secretary, deserves special thanks for typing and retyping pages of manuscript.

My thanks to my chief helper and main source of encouragement, Wendy, my wife. I found a good thing!

Finally my thanks to my children, Ben, Anna, Joel, Simon, and Timothy, for their patience throughout my long sessions in the study.

CONTENTS

CONTENTS

FOREWORD

*I*t was in the late sixties that groups of Christians seeking the restoration of the church began to surface in Britain. To the casual observer the prominent feature was that Christians were worshiping in their homes rather than in traditional church buildings. It was almost inevitable that this should become known as "the house-church movement."

On two counts this was something of a misnomer. In the first place, the use of the home for worship was not the root of this tree of God's planting, but was only one of the minor branches. As far as the use of the home is concerned, leaders had rejected the "consecrated building" concept, in the conviction that:

Where'er they seek thee thou art found,
And every place is hallowed ground.

They also saw that meeting in the home was not only a New Testament practice, but that it had great practical advantages over the formal church setting, especially where numbers were small.

"House-church movement" is a misnomer, secondly, because there was no sense in which the home was viewed as sacrosanct, as far as the gathering of the church was concerned. Consequently, as the churches grew—and they did so with rapidity—there was no problem in moving to more commodious buildings, such as schools, community centers, town halls, or even unused church buildings. When this happened, the congregation still retained the home setting for the smaller home groups that met midweek, having discovered the great value of these smaller settings.

Soon traditional churches of the more progressive variety were following suit, breaking down into smaller groups meeting in the homes midweek for Bible study, prayer, and fellowship. Thus home meetings became even less a distinctive feature of the "house-church movement."

If the use of the home is but a branch of this tree, what is the root? In a word, it is a diligent attempt to restore the church to New Testament Christianity, both in principle and in practice. Behind all that you will read in this book is the deep conviction that God has not left us without witness as to how He would have His house ordered. The New Testament provides us with principles, with examples, and with corrective teaching, but not with an inflexible pattern or blueprint.

The author makes no boast that he has covered it all or that he knows it all. "God is continually widening our horizons," he says. He would be the first to admit that what has been discovered is not being perfectly implemented. We are all frail, finite vessels who stand in continual need of the grace of God.

I want to commend this book wholeheartedly for a number of reasons. In the first place, Terry Virgo is a close friend and colleague, and I know that his life and ministry is in itself a practical demonstration of what he writes about. He does not speak from theory but from experience. He shares with great candor his own inner struggles as he sought to follow God's leading in those early years, and to bring a congregation for which he was responsible into the freedom of life in the Spirit. What he has raised up under God in the church in Hove, in the United Kingdom and in many other congregations bears eloquent testimony to what he advocates.

The second reason is that what Terry sets forth is now being demonstrated in many other parts of the world. When we find restoration-type churches that have quite independently discovered the same truths and have begun to operate on the same basis, we can only conclude that this is the spontaneous working of God.

It follows directly from this that restoration principles are proving to be not only biblical, but also successful. Where almost all denominational churches in the United Kingdom are showing serious decline in numbers, and others are struggling to keep their chins above water, restoration-type churches, without any central headquarters, and involving many different streams and emphases, are growing by leaps and bounds. The fastest church growth in the world—some believe the fastest in the history of the church—is in the house-church movement of China. And the fact that it has had no connection with house churches outside of that land simply emphasizes once again that we are seeing a worldwide movement of the Holy Spirit.

I pray that God will use this book to cause many to face questions from which they might naturally shrink, such as, "What is God saying to His people through these new churches?" and, "What does He want us to do about it?"

— *Arthur Wallis*

CHAPTER 1

Come and See

*"I*f I become a Christian do I have to go in there?" The boy was pointing at the church next door. We had transformed the church hall into a coffee bar that looked like a barn. Straw carpeted the floor, and boxes and bales of hay served as tables and chairs. A relaxed and welcoming atmosphere had been created, and local young people had flocked in.

Two young men I was speaking to had become very interested in the gospel, but here was the great stumbling block: Would they have to go to church if they became Christians? The gospel of the Lord Jesus had become a gripping reality, but the thought of "going in there" appalled them. As a zealous young evangelist I replied, "Don't look at the church; look at Jesus."

What a contradiction to the prayer of Jesus that the world, seeing the glory of the church, might believe that the Father had sent him. However, I was in an era and a situation where the church was no advertisement for the gospel. It was easier to concentrate on having a "personal Savior" and then trying to find "the church of your choice."

We did not talk about the church in those days. Somehow it seemed as irrelevant to us as it did to the outsider. Mick Jagger of the Rolling Stones is reported to have said, "Jesus Christ was fantastic, but I do not like the church. The church does more harm than good." As an evangelist, I saw that evangelism was not the biggest problem of the church, but rather that the church was the biggest hindrance to evangelism.

Halfway house

In the days when coffee house evangelism was the thing, conferences were held to discuss the problem of bridging the awful gulf between the coffee bar and the communion table. Some even proposed a halfway house, where people could be prepared for church life. How could lively, modern young people be trained to cope with dead, irrelevant, formal church services? How could we tell them that this cold, unchanging monotony was the body of Christ enjoying abundant life? Few were fooled and few were added, and many an evangelist broke his heart.

Zeal for God's house

It was said of Jesus: "Zeal for Your house will consume me." That zeal was demonstrated in no uncertain way as animals fled from His scourge and money-changers searched the floor for their scattered coins (John 2:13-17, NIV). Do we have zeal for God's house, or do we see the church as a hopeless anachronism? Many Christians would reply, "Of course we go to church," but that wasn't my question. Do we have zeal for God's house?

Jesus, with all the controlled passion that enabled him to set His face and go to Jerusalem, confidently declared: "I will build my church; and the gates of hell shall not prevail against it" (Matt. 16:18, AV). He is determined to have a spotless bride that has made herself ready for marriage to the Lamb. "Ah," you answer, "this is the universal church that no man can number, not just a local assembly." Certainly there is truth in that, but should we therefore expect the local assembly to be in such contrast to this marvelous spiritual body?

The Book of Revelation shows Jesus, not as one who is vaguely in the midst of the church, but as one who walks among the individual lamp stands. He knows each local church inti-

mately. He commends one and warns another. He notes stead-
fastness here, apathy there. Each is an open book to Him. His
longing for a glorious bride is seen in His concern and ambition
for each particular congregation. How far short we come in our
attitude to the local church! Our devotion to Christ is rarely
matched by a similar devotion to His church, but finds expression
in other areas. And so we fail to share God's heart and follow His
strategy.

It is easy to sympathize with those whose evangelistic zeal
causes them to turn in frustration from the local church to start
an evangelism society. But in the end, we are forced to see that
God wants a building, not just a pile of bricks, and, until
foundational issues are settled, new bricks add to the problem.

Paul did not work simply to win converts, but to plant
churches as well. He did not regard his evangelizing work as
complete until elders had been established and churches formed.
It was through the local church that the kingdom of God was to
be manifested. From them the gospel should sound forth.

Moving in charismatic circles

In the recent so-called "charismatic movement" many have
encountered God in a new way, leading to an experience of
spiritual gifts. Sadly, this has often resulted in the mushrooming
of non-church activity. Instead of local churches welcoming this
new energy, many have shut their doors to the charismatic gifts,
forcing people into an unscriptural situation. While remaining
loyal to their churches on Sunday, many attend mid-week
meetings for charismatic fellowship. Hence their energies are
squandered and the church fails to benefit. If these groups are
without proper oversight they become open to error, so the
whole strategy of God for the church to contain and oversee
spiritual life is frustrated.

Such a mid-week meeting can be regarded as a prop while
people endure the Sunday services. So we produce Christians
who have divided loyalties; neither group receives their wholehearted support. Because the mid-week meeting is only "a

fellowship" with no pastor—not a church—no one actually has the care of their souls or enjoys the full weight of their commitment. While expressing loyalty to their original church they in fact dissipate their energies, and their church leaders' suspicions are aroused. Also, the question must be faced: Do we take our newly converted friends to the prayer group or to the church we attend on Sundays?

There is no doubt about it—the baptism of the Holy Spirit spells trouble whether we seek it or not! But why should that be so? Many have condemned the whole "charismatic movement" by arguing that the Holy Spirit is not the author of division, and they feel, therefore, that the whole thing can be written off since division seems to abound.

"Keep it to yourself!"

Some argue, "You can have your spiritual gifts, but please keep them to yourselves"; however, this is impossible. The simple point is that "each one is given the manifestation of the Spirit for the common good" (1 Cor. 12:7). In other words, the gifts of the Holy Spirit are to be shared. They only operate among people who want to receive gifts from one another. Such gifts as prophecies, healing, tongues, and interpretations have to be manifested.

At this point decisions have to be made by every individual. If my present church says no to the gifts of the Holy Spirit, what should I do? Shall I simply forget this experience? Shall I say it is of secondary importance? Shall I stay, therefore, and keep it to myself? Perhaps I should stay and try to influence change in this church. I could start speaking to others and start a weekly charismatic prayer meeting. But then will I form a clique? Should I leave and be disloyal to my pastor or my vicar and friends? Where would I go?

People have been wrestling with such painful questions for two decades now. Others have been privileged to belong to churches whose leaders have made the radical changes necessary to respond to this new life. Changing a traditional church into a flexible new wineskin is no easy matter. It takes great singleness of purpose, patience, love, and faith. It will not be accomplished without pain and heartache.

Some traditional churches are more open to change than others. Local independence makes it possible for some to make the transformation, providing there is a willing congregation. Others set out on the path of renewal only to encounter immovable objects deeply rooted in the denomination's tradition. They either proceed through a very difficult period of change, or they reach the "denominational ceiling" and stop. Where there is failure to make fundamental changes, churches usually revert to their former ways; and the "renewal" fades into the background.

New churches emerging

The fact remains that all over the world new-style churches of growing significance are emerging. Some came to birth through a small group who pulled up their roots and started meeting elsewhere, perhaps in a home. Others are churches that have gone through a period of painful change from within. Very often they have lost some members who did not want change. Now, having weathered the storms, they are beginning to emerge in health, providing an ideal base from which evangelism can flourish. Warm, loving communities with stirring worship and united purpose provide a healthy home for new converts, of whom many are beginning to be saved and added.

There is a so-called "movement" in the church today. In England, the most common name for it is the "house-church movement." The "house-church" title seems to signify that the meeting place is all-important, but in fact this is a matter of very little relevance. I mentioned this once in an interview with a Christian magazine, but the intrepid interviewer would not be put off the scent. "There is something different about the churches you represent," he said, "even when they meet in conventional church buildings."

That is true. And here lies the motivation for this book. There are many ways in which such a book could be written. For instance, a historical account might be interesting; but that is not my purpose. I want rather to share some of the vision and burden commonly felt by so many within the "movement." Having said that, the vision set forth in this book represents only one viewpoint and makes no pretense of being the final word on the matter.

No headquarters

In spite of the frequent rumors, there is no headquarters, no front office to lay down company policy. As in God's natural creation, so here there is great diversity, but there are common principles and a deep desire to be one body in Christ.

Churches seeking restoration are led by evangelical believers with very orthodox, Bible-believing backgrounds. They do not conceal wild fanatics, nor are they exclusive and authoritarian sects; they are simply Christians trying to be obedient to the Spirit and His Word. They may have made many mistakes on their journey; often they seemed like the young Joseph after he saw his visions and dreamed his dreams. Where there is adolescent zeal, God has His ways of training. But in the main, these churches consist of people who have come to a fresh experience of the Holy Spirit which has not left them complacently claiming superiority, but has whetted their appetites for more of God and His ways, and they are endeavoring to build churches where He is free to move.

I thank God for an evangelical background where the importance of the Word of God was emphasized, but where there was also the call to a life empowered by the Holy Spirit. As a young convert I read the biographies of many who had sought and found God in powerful ways. Their experience of the Holy Spirit made me very hungry for more.

Throughout the sixties and seventies, a great number of people have been filled with the Holy Spirit and have sought to be obedient to the repercussions of that experience. When they came seeking they had no idea where it would lead them. I, for one, had no realization that receiving the Holy Spirit and experiencing charismatic renewal would have such far-reaching implications. I simply longed to receive power that I might be a better witness for Jesus.

Many sought a new experience of the Holy Spirit purely out of a sense of personal need. What they actually received was more than they expected. It was as though a line of dominoes had been set up and someone had pushed the one on the end. They found that the outworkings of their experience had immediate implications for church life. Can we be flexible enough to let the new life express itself? Will the whole thing run riot if we take the brakes off? How willing are we for change?

Follow Maker's instructions

Jeremiah's prophetic call was to pluck up and to break down as well as to build and to plant. This radical surgery is required first of all in our inner attitudes. We must never settle, as did Israel in Haggai's day, for this statement: "The time has not come . . . for the house of the Lord to be rebuilt" (Hag. 1·2). If God is pouring out His Spirit, let us have faith to build His house aright. We often read, "For best results follow the maker's instructions," and the Bible does not leave us ignorant as to how the church should function.

God has ordained a strategy. He is building a church. The apostles, as wise master builders and stewards of the mysteries of Christ, followed the vision by giving top priority to planting local churches. The church is God's answer to crumbling society. May God deliver us from leaving her as an anachronism to be ignored by the world and the Christian alike; rather, may we see her as the pearl of great price, the bride for which Jesus gave all.

As we see the church moving into renewal and restoration we can, with growing confidence, not only tell people to look away to Jesus, but can even invite them along to "come and see."

But what is actually happening in these churches that are seeking restoration? Trying to phone the headquarters of the movement would pose quite a problem; and, in an age when churches around the globe can share their ideas quite freely, it would be very difficult to trace the movement's growth. What is happening at the grass roots?

Many would be surprised if they moved within the ranks, asking people what fresh truths they had embraced and what experiences made them value their new-found church life.

"I think the thing we appreciate most is the laughter," testified one who has recently joined such a church. Her letter continued, "David is just overjoyed to be with the men—it is what he has needed for years."

Personal restoration

The message of restoration is not exclusively about the restoration of apostolic and prophetic gifts, though we regard these as vital. Structural changes do not dominate our thinking. We long to see people coming into the full wealth of their potential in Christ.

Many evangelicals are rendered ineffective by a sense of personal rejection. The gospel has not yet freed them from their apparent insignificance. Though they thank God for forgiveness of sins and the promise of heaven, they do not seem to be fundamentally changed people. Many remain bound by hidden fears and insecurities that make them vulnerable to envy, jealousy, and other such spiritual sicknesses.

Changing our meetings and structures will achieve little if individual members are not personally well established in Christ. They need to sense their personal worth. They must abandon wrong foundations in order to build on the only foundation that will survive the storms. They need a life-changing revelation of the grace of God that does not leave them tied up in knots of legalism. Then, having received their own personal outpouring of the Holy Spirit, they rejoice in the radical changes in church life that are taking place.

My early chapters reflect this conviction as I focus initially on the restoration of the individual, before considering the broader implications for the local church.

CHAPTER 2

Chosen for Fruit

I was asked to speak at the nurses' fellowship, and the topic they gave me was, "Why am I a Christian?"

As I began to prepare for the meeting I realized they were looking for an approach which showed why I had chosen Christianity. Perhaps I could say I had tried everything else first but found life so empty; perhaps I could argue against the other philosophies and religions and then extol the virtues of Christianity. As I pondered I could see that neither of these approaches would honestly answer the question.

The Sunday before the meeting, about a dozen people were baptized at my home church, a large Baptist church. As was the custom, they all gave their testimonies before being baptized. Then, as each entered the pool, the pastor gave him a Bible text.

The converts offered a variety of reasons for "choosing Christ," but the final text given by the pastor was the true answer to the question. As the nervous candidate stood in the pool with 700 people silently waiting for the text, the truth rang out: "You did not choose Me, but I chose you, and appointed you, that you should go and bear fruit, and that your fruit should remain" (John 15:16).

That was it! That was why I was a Christian. That would be my text for the nurses. God had chosen me. It would not be true to say that I had first researched other religions and seen the superiority of Christianity. Neither was it true that I had come to the end of myself and needed an answer. Certainly I had been searching for some answers, but the night I was converted was an ordinary Saturday night. My sister had returned home, recently saved, and had led me to Christ. Prior to that I had been a fairly happy teenager, enjoying life to the full, not an earnest seeker after God and truth.

In the end we are believers because we are a chosen people. Our roots precede our "decision for Christ" and go back to God's eternal choice. This is true for every believer. Together we make up a chosen people.

But who am I to call myself chosen? Why did God choose me? In the end the whole thing is a mystery. The New Testament gives us some answers, but they are the very opposite of what we would expect.

Only the best?

We would expect God to choose the wise, the noble, the strong, especially when we realize He has a great purpose for His church. After all, He wants to reveal His glory to the world and to principalities and powers, so surely He would choose only the very best.

Amazingly, He turns the whole issue upside down. He does not choose many wise, but has preferred the foolish (1 Cor. 1:26-29). This whole book may prove a problem to "wise" people, but I trust that God's chosen "foolish things of the world" will rejoice in it. So often those who are not bright feel very threatened by their lack of gray matter; but it is exciting to discover that God, in His sovereignty, has chosen to hide these things from the clever and reveal them to babes. Some clever people may be privileged to be included in the purposes of God, but they will only really enjoy all His purposes if they humble themselves and become as little children.

But surely God needs strong, dynamic people? No, He does not choose many mighty. Some who are mighty will be included, but not many. Moses was mighty as a young man. He was mighty in word and deed—quite a guy, in fact! He was even willing to discard all his riches and fame in order to identify with the despised Hebrew slaves. What a breakthrough! Think of his power and prestige now added to the cause. Strangely, God did not seem to see it that way. In fact Moses was a chosen one, but God first had to drain every last vestige of arrogant self-confidence from him before he could be used. Moses volunteered "young, strong, and free, to be the best that he could be" only to find that God required other qualifications before he could be useful. In Moses' case, it took forty years to reach that stage of usefulness.

Those who have been ashamed of their humble origins can rejoice that not many noble have been chosen because the base have been preferred. Children of suspect marriages, like Solomon, are preferred above their legitimate half-brothers. Even the despised and rejected are chosen, and the things that "are not."

David "was not"

Samuel, the national prophet, arrived at Jesse's home asking to see all his sons (1 Sam. 16:1-3). They were duly summoned and stood magnificently in a row, all seven of them shining and bright—a credit to their father. Strangely, Samuel heard no inner confirmation that any of them were God's choice. How could this be? Hadn't he heard clearly from God after all?

"Are these all your children?" he probed.

"No, there is one more. He is just looking after the sheep."

It was as though David had not existed in Jesse's eyes when Samuel asked to see his sons. Given the opportunity to display his fine sons to the highly respected Samuel, he had completely overlooked David. David's own brothers also seemed to have a contemptuous attitude toward him. But God had chosen the one that "was not" in order to bring to naught a certain Goliath, who very much was!

Who are we? We are God's chosen people. Not the arrogant

elite, but weak, foolish, base, and despised—the poor in spirit
who have been promised the kingdom of heaven, the meek who
will inherit the earth, often all too aware of their weakness and
vulnerability. Many of us battle with difficult backgrounds and
childhood experiences which seem to disqualify us. We wrestle
with poor self-image and problems of rejection that cripple our
usefulness to God. But if God has specially selected those who
seem disqualified, we can take courage. More than that, we can
ask why He has saved us. What was His purpose?

At the end of his life David earned the enviable testimony that
he had "served the purpose of God in his own generation" (Acts
13:36). He laid hold of that for which God had laid hold of him.
Every child of God is a child of destiny; God has laid hold of you
for a purpose. This is what makes each believer unique and
precious and gives your life a glorious dignity.

We are not simply people who decided to follow Jesus, nor
did we stumble into the kingdom of God through random events.
God chose us and had a specific role for us to fulfill in His plan.
He chose us that we might bear fruit. We must beware, therefore,
of hiding behind our sense of insignificance, or we might miss the
destiny God has for us. Part of the message of restoration is the
recovery of the sense of purpose for every believer.

Identity crisis

Many Christians suffer from an identity crisis. When congratu-
lated for a job well done, when giving a public testimony, for
instance, they say, "It wasn't me; it was the Lord." When you
reply, "But I'm sure I saw your lips moving," they insist, "Oh, you
know what I mean." But do we really know? Often, while desiring
to give the Lord the glory, we are not sure where we personally
fit in. We reject any praise for fear of robbing God of His due. This
is a legitimate concern, but we need to clarify our thinking. Are
we mere puppets in God's hands?

Drain-pipes only, blessed Master,
But with all Thy wondrous power
Flowing through us . . .?

The danger is that we can so overstate the case that we are left entirely without identity or significance. Should it be our highest aim to be hidden from view so that Jesus might be glorified? Is this really what God wants of us? I recall a preacher warning that if another deacon prayed before a meeting, "Lord, hide the preacher this morning. May we see Jesus only," he would assist by dropping down behind the pulpit!

Though Paul was meticulous about not seeking glory from men, he did not hesitate to invite others to be imitators of him. He would not have endorsed the sentiments of the modern bumper sticker, "Don't Follow Me, Follow Jesus." He boldly pointed to himself as one to be followed. "What you have learned and received and heard and seen in me, do; and the God of peace will be with you" (Phil. 4:9, RSV).

"Lost in God"

Sometimes we encounter those who express the longing to be "lost in God." However, God is not calling us to lose ourselves, but rather to stand up and be counted. God is very interested in personal identity. When Jerusalem was rebuilt it was certainly God who wrought the work, as the heathen were quick to perceive (Neh. 6:16). Yet Scripture records in verse after verse the names of those who actually built the walls. It is oriental religion that invites its devotees to lose themselves in what they worship.

Jesus warned us that the thief comes to steal, kill, and destroy, and if he can rob us of our identity and destroy our individuality, he will do it. God, who created our individuality, is concerned to preserve it that we might have a relationship of developing maturity with Him. Beware a "lost in God" mentality that appears to release you from individual accountability.

Ultimately we must all appear before the judgment seat of Christ in order that each one may be judged by what he has done in the body (2 Cor. 5:10). Each will give account of himself to God (Rom. 14:10-12). The account we give will be not whether we asked Jesus to be our Savior or whether our doctrine was pure, but what we have done in the body. "The Son of Man is going to come in the glory of His Father with His angels, and He will then recompense every man according to his deeds" (Matt. 16:27). Nothing will be hidden on that day (Luke 12:2-3). Do not suppose this is only for the unbeliever.

Fire test

There will come a day when our works will be tested by fire (1 Cor. 3:13-15). Jesus gave us a sample of such testing when he stood at the temple watching people bringing their gifts. The rich man's vast gifts and the widow's two mites both experienced the test of the fiery gaze of Jesus. The former were burned up, but the mites were spiritually transformed into precious stones by the test of fire.

Paul tells us that when the Lord comes He will bring to light the things hidden in darkness and disclose the motives of men's hearts, and then each man's praise will come to him from God (1 Cor. 4:5). There will be an accountability, not only of action but of motivation. That which is not motivated by love will profit us nothing (1 Cor. 13:3). Thus some will "suffer loss" when the fire tries their work and it is burned up, though they themselves will be saved. Their eternal redemption is secure because this is by the grace of God. It was in a time of revival, as is often the case, that God's heavenly standard brought the works of Ananias and Sapphira to the test and they suffered loss (Acts 5:1-11). They were no doubt personally saved but only "as through the fire."

Jesus taught that we are to be like men waiting for their master, living responsibly in the light of His return and ready at any moment to give account.

All this underlines the importance of being fully committed to a living church where accountability is part of the discipleship training one receives. Intimate fellowship and the discipling of our lives help us to be accountable to one another. Group leaders work with church elders who will themselves give account to God, not only for their own lives but also for the souls over which they are keeping watch (Heb. 13:17). Practical accountability in the present prepares us for the great day of giving account and helps to deliver us from spiritual unreality.

Our calling is both a privilege and a responsibility. Paul was not content to play at religion or to merely keep the ecclesiastical wheels turning. He was running a race, fighting a fight, and at the end he could confidently say, "Henceforth there is laid up for me the crown of righteousness which the Lord, the righteous judge, will award to me on that day" (2 Tim. 4:8, RSV). God had bestowed on him His grace, and Paul was determined that that grace would not be in vain (1 Cor. 15:10).

God has given us his grace, too. He has called us by name and given us identity. As we face the responsibility of serving the purpose of God in our generation, we need always to keep before us the promise of our Lord Jesus, who did not hesitate to encourage His disciples with promises of rewards at His coming. "I am coming quickly, and My reward is with Me, to render to every man according to what he has done" (Rev. 22:12).

Christians have invented an ethic higher than that of the Bible when they say they are "not looking for any reward save that of knowing they do God's will." Part of the message of restoration is to bring back the reality of accountability and the wonder of working for the purpose of gathering fruit unto eternal life. As a result, all our Christian activity must come under scrutiny to see whether it is merely a dead work, devoid of faith and based only on tradition, or truly a living work of love, faith, and hope, full of purpose that will certainly bear fruit for God.

God chose each one of us before the foundation of the world. He delights in us as His dear children. Though we often see ourselves as weak, God proclaims, "Let the weak say 'I am a mighty man'" (Joel 3:10). Assured of His faithfulness, we must go on to do the works "prepared beforehand, that we should walk in them" (Eph. 2:10), looking with anticipation for the reward that comes to those who have proved faithful and fruitful.

CHAPTER 3

Right Foundations

"*B*ut Lord, why did You let him go? He's influential and rich, he came and acknowledged You humbly, he asked about eternal life, and now he's walking away. Surely You could have talked to him about a right attitude toward his money later on?" But Jesus let the rich young ruler go, knowing that life cannot be built on a wrong foundation. Jesus was never afraid to introduce a negative note before announcing good news. His kingdom manifesto, the mighty Sermon on the Mount, begins with a blessing for those who mourn and are poor in spirit—not exactly "the power of positive thinking"!

Before we can build lives that glorify God and survive storms, we must be careful to pull down and destroy the rubbish upon which our lives were previously built. Before Christ becomes our rock, we all trust in something else. It may be our money, our willpower, our humor and charm, or perhaps our intellectual ability. Whatever it is must be replaced by a living faith in Christ.

The storms of life all too frequently reveal that after conversion Christians are still actually building their lives on the wrong foundation. What looked secure in the sunshine is exposed as hopelessly inadequate when overtaken by the tempest. How can we avoid the all-too-familiar sight of Christians, who previously seemed to be progressing well, collapsing in adversity? Like Jesus, we must pull down before we build up.

Self-sufficient?

Self-confidence has to undergo major surgery if we are to be safe in the kingdom of God. Our heavenly Father does not want a family of fearful, insecure children, but He does want our confidence to be built on His own faithfulness and power, not on our own ability. When we trust our own strength we may find, like Moses, that we are able to destroy one Egyptian, but coping with the Red Sea is another matter altogether. When we are truly living by faith, no burden need be larger than another because each is genuinely cast upon God, who sustains us throughout.

Those who are naturally strong find the kingdom of God a stumbling block. They withstand everyday pressures easily, and so their lack of faith in God is not manifest until they encounter the apparently impossible situation. Suddenly they find their resources have run out: they are unable to cope. Only then do they discover that they were not living as branches abiding in the Vine at all.

We often fail to believe two important Bible statements: Jesus' words, " . . . apart from Me you can do nothing" (John 15:5), and the promise that "nothing will be impossible with God" (Luke 1:37). Instead, we live in a middle area of human ability. We still draw on our own resources as mere men. Here the strong and extroverted shine, while the weak and introverted are left behind. God's desire for us is to be like Gideon "whose weakness was turned to strength" by faith (Heb. 11:34, NIV). His purpose is to change us from one degree of glory to another. He is not content to save our souls but leave our lifestyles unchanged.

We dare not build on our natural foundations; we must make a fresh start like Zacchaeus, no longer living by his wits but by faith in Jesus and obedience to His laws. Check right now: On what foundation are you building your life? What principles affect the big decisions of your life and your present impact for Christ in the world and in the church? We all know the jargon, but are our lives truly built on the words of Jesus?

The root of the problem

God gave man an instinct for self-preservation. As with natural appetites such as hunger, thirst, and sexual desire, there is nothing inherently evil in this instinct. It is built into our makeup to ensure the survival and reproduction of the species. At the Fall, however, man's whole character was horribly contorted, and this natural instinct became warped into gross self-interest, manifested throughout society by the philosophy of "looking after number one."

When I was converted, this self-interest never received the fatal blow that would have come through deep repentance. Instead I began to build a shaky Christian life by asking Jesus into this now divided heart. So started years of inner conflict which were only concluded by heartbreak and collapse. This ultimately led to laying the foundation which should have been laid at the beginning. Years had been wasted.

We can no more build a Christian life on a foundation of self-interest than we can build a house on sand, yet how often people are encouraged to do just that. Repeatedly they are simply invited to ask Jesus into their hearts or believe that Jesus died for their sins. Our Lord was unafraid to publish very unpalatable terms of discipleship when He called men to follow Him. He went right to the root of the problem at the outset, proclaiming, "If anyone wishes to come after Me, let him deny himself, and take up his cross, and follow Me. For whoever wishes to save his life shall lose it; and whoever loses his life for My sake and the gospel's shall save it" (Mark 8:34-35).

"Taking up the cross" does not mean enduring aches and pains, as it is often interpreted. A man seen carrying a cross in Jesus' day had only a few hours to live. When Jesus invited men to take up the cross He was asking them to lay down their lives. Following Christ involves losing one's life, which is why it begins with a burial service in baptism.

Being baptized is not something that a new Christian can do or not do, as he pleases. It demonstrates the burial of the old self, which is part of conversion. The Bible gives us no authority to preach forgiveness of sins and eternal life without reference to baptism and all that it signifies. From the beginning we are not our own; we have been bought for a price. As Walter Chantry says, "We have no right to lower Jesus' entry requirements for His kingdom. Christ has not invented a different gospel for the twentieth century."[1] Having then laid this foundation, we must ensure that our lives are built lastingly upon it.

Signs of self-interest

How can we discover if the root problem has been dealt with adequately ? There are several manifestations of self-interest that betray one's true situation.

1. "It's not fair"

A Christian who always demands his "rights" has never understood the cross. We should rejoice that God has not given us what we justly deserve. If He had, we would still be without Him and without hope, coming under fearful judgment. As it is, God has dealt with us in mercy and has caused grace to overflow toward us. Our inconsistency is revealed when, having entered through the door marked "Grace," we then demand justice when we are inside. God has never promised us this kind of deal. He orders our lives "according to the mystery of His will," not according to our understanding of fair play. Therefore things will often happen to us that seem unjust. If we have not laid down our lives and embraced the cross we shall be offended by every difficulty we face.

Stephen was stoned and died. Paul was stoned and raised up. James died in prison but Peter was miraculously delivered. It's not fair, but no one said it would be fair. God does not bow and cringe before another, higher throne inscribed with the shining words "Fair Play." There is no higher authority that calls Him into line. He does all things after the counsel of His own will, and receives counsel from no one else. He is almighty.

Indignant believers who claim that they are going to ask God to explain certain apparent injustices when they get to glory are in for a shock. Their attitude may well be the fruit of an evangelism that begins and ends with man and his desire for fulfillment, promising peace and joy if only we will ask Jesus into our lives. Some are even exhorted to "give Jesus a chance." Such preaching only leads to trouble because it panders to "almighty man," instead of bringing him to his knees in deep humility and repentance.

Paul responds to "Is it fair?" with another question: "Who are you, O man, who answers back to God?. . . Does not the potter have a right over the clay. . . ?" (Rom. 9:20-21). We must learn that God is the righteous judge of all the earth, and if He pleases to employ men in the morning, at noon, or at the end of the day, and then pay them all the same wages, it is not for us to question His wisdom or righteousness. We can only worship, giving Him thanks that He called us to serve Him at all. A murmuring and complaining tongue displays a faulty foundation and shows that not enough was pulled down before building began.

2. "Self" in religious disguise

If selfish motivation is not radically uprooted it can creep into the very heart of our Christian activity and aspiration. We can be involved in all manner of Christian work in order to feed and justify the self. I have to acknowledge that my earliest endeavors at door-to-door and street evangelism were more for my own sake than for the hearers'. I felt good at the end of the day, not because anyone had been saved, but because I had proved myself. A little persecution made it even more worthwhile. When Jesus went to the cross, though, it was not to justify Himself but to justify us.

Prayer meetings with confessions of how unworthy we are and how we long to be made worthy can be the breeding ground for a wrong attitude toward self. The gospel tells us that we are worthy only of condemnation and death. The good news is that Jesus took our guilt and condemnation and that God accepts us freely just as we are, without strength or worth. But this is so humbling. We long to prove our own worth. Like the Jews of Paul's day we want to establish a righteousness of our own, instead of rejoicing in the righteousness God has given us as a free gift.

Grace is always humbling, but if we will accept God's judgment and gladly embrace His free gift, we need never strive to resurrect that old self and make it worthy. By all means let us perfect holiness in the fear of God, but let us do so from the right foundation. To build again what we once destroyed would be a tragedy (Gal. 2:18).

3. *Poor me!*

Perhaps the saddest manifestation of self and the clearest proof that there is more pulling down to be done is when self-pity raises its ugly head. If the devil finds all other approaches closed he loves to try this one. "Nobody really cares about you," he whispers in your ear. "Nobody would notice if you were missing; you haven't got a real friend in the whole church." How easily we get caught when we are feeling low. Self-pity rises to the surface like a fish to bait. First we enjoy its taste; then we find an ugly hook piercing our spirit: bitterness springs up, spoiling relationships and robbing us of our joy in God.

Jesus showed no trace of self-pity when Satan tempted Him in the wilderness, nor when He carried His own cross to Golgotha. Even from the cross His thoughts were for others. The invitation to take up our cross and follow Him involves a call to a similar stance of selflessness. There must be a deliberate refusal to be drawn by the sirens of self-pity, however attractive and sympathetic their songs may seem. They lead only to destructive rocks which are able to inflict untold damage.

The call to follow Christ involves a deliberate decision to refuse self, and we can only accomplish this by faith. We must believe that God's judgment on our self-centeredness is right and then abide by it. We must then go on to believe that we can leave everything with God. He genuinely loves us, and orders all things for our good. So we begin to build on a right foundation.

Until we are rooted and grounded in love there will be no genuine growth. We may learn new words and doctrines, but spiritual growth will be continually frustrated. We will begin to build; then our self-interest will be threatened, and we will either retaliate, demanding our rights, or be overwhelmed with remorse and hurt.

Impossible without faith

A genuine trust in our heavenly Father's love and ability to look after us is vital if we are going to build our lives aright. It is by keeping ourselves in the love of God that we provide a base for building ourselves up in our faith (Jude 20-21). When Jesus was tempted to act from self-interest He overcame by never questioning His Father's love and power. Even with Pilate mocking Him, He was assured that the governor had no authority over Him unless His Father permitted it (John 19:10-11). Jesus had no need to fight for Himself. He had total confidence in His Father and was totally committed to His will, even though it included the cross.

It is only by unswerving faith that we can walk as Jesus walked. Knowing that wicked men had placed Him in Rome's cruel grasp never made Him retaliate. He was reigning in the midst of adversity; His foundation was secure. Jesus repeatedly tested the stability of His apostles. Would they trust Him on a stormy lake? Would they flounder when asked to feed the thousands? Repeatedly they collapsed in unbelief and fear, but ultimately His purpose was accomplished in them.

Take Peter, for example. He had come a long way without a proper foundation. He had been with Jesus for three years, witnessing His mighty works and profound words, and had himself healed the sick and cast out demons. He had discovered his need of Jesus when, walking on the water, he began to sink. Yet at the time of Jesus' arrest he was still trusting in himself.

Though others might fail the Lord, he would not. How painful was Peter's fall, but how he needed it!

The rock-like qualities that Jesus wanted to be manifested in Peter's life were not to be based on his own bravado but on the grace and faithfulness of his Lord. Peter was never the same again. Later his faith faced the ultimate challenge. In prison, about to die, he had no plans to escape. He was not complaining that he had barely begun his apostolic ministry. He was not asking, "Why me?" Instead, like Jesus in the storm on the lake, he was fast asleep, and the delivering angel had to waken him (Acts 12:7). God had triumphed in his unstable life. Now his house was on the rock.

The tragedy of wrong foundations is that they are discovered at such cost. They are hidden from view and only revealed in times of great pressure. The house may be an impressive structure with attractive decorations, but outward appearances can be very deceptive. We can even deceive ourselves—the most dangerous deception of all.

How do you know if you are on rock or sand? It's simple. The foundation of your life is the hidden part. Only you and God know about it. Do adverse circumstances shake your faith to the roots, or do you believe in a God who can use them to His glory? Do you still obey God when no one else is looking or only when other Christians are present? Is there any difference between your public and private conduct? Do you do things in secret that you would never want another Christian to know about? If so, beware! Dig deep and put your house on the rock of obedience. Only those who do are truly God's disciples.

CHAPTER 4

Amazing Grace

*R*estoration in the church is not simply a matter of charismatic gifts and new church structures. The people of God must be restored to a fresh appreciation of all that is theirs in Christ. Freedom from law and condemnation open the door for praise and wholehearted dedication to God.

Sadly, many a Christian is more aware of a sense of failure and condemnation than of reigning and rejoicing. If we are going to see the church restored we must first see individuals breaking out of the legalism that often pervades the atmosphere of evangelicalism.

"Amazing Grace" is more than the title of a grand old hymn that has been given a face-lift and even reached the pop charts. For many of us, once steeped in the "do's and don'ts" of evangelical tradition, it has become a glorious, liberating secret. We have at last heard the unqualified statement of our absolute freedom from law, which is the very heart of the gospel. The temptation to reduce our Christian experience to the mere observance of

external regulations has yielded to the authority of God's Word:
"For under the Law I 'died,' and I am dead to the Law's demands
so that I may live for God" (Gal. 2:19, Phillips).

A different gospel

Nothing has hindered the growth of the kingdom more than the
ugly face of legalism. The devil realizes that undermining the very
character of the gospel is far more effective than opposing it
blatantly, because he then reduces it to the level of an irrelevant
religion. A piety consisting of "Don't handle, don't taste, don't
touch!" may have the appearance of wisdom in self-made religion
(NASB margin: "delight in religiousness"), but Paul tells the
Colossians it is of no value against fleshly indulgence (Col. 2:21-
23). It is at least comforting to know that Paul faced the same kind
of problem in the first century. He was amazed that his followers
had so quickly deserted "Him who called you by the grace of
Christ, for a different gospel; which is really not another; only
there are some who . . . want to distort the gospel of Christ" (Gal.
1:6-7).

Having told the Romans that they are freely justified and
declared righteous as a gift "apart from the law," Paul replies to
the obvious question that such a statement raises—namely,
"What about the law, then?" In Romans 7, Paul explains that by
nature we are all married to the law. He is a hard, unrelenting
husband. We are totally under his authority, and he is constantly
pointing out our errors and shortcomings. Not only does he show
us our faults and remind us of his standards, but he never lifts a
finger to help us. He is impotent to help. One further thing about
this overbearing husband is that he is always right. What a
husband! We are married to him for life; and there is, according
to Romans 7, no freedom to marry another, since this would be
a form of adultery.

Just to quench any last glimmer of hope on the horizon, Jesus
quite plainly taught that the law would never pass away (Matt.
5:17-20). We seem to be permanently trapped in a marriage with

a fault-finding, overbearing, meticulously correct husband who cannot actually help us and who also prevents us from marrying a new husband. Condemnation looms large.

The way out

Is there no escape? Having painted the blackest possible picture, Paul goes on to show us the way out. The law will never die, but—glorious truth!—we were made to die to the law through the body of Christ, that we might be joined to another, to Him who is raised from the dead (Rom. 7:4).

God reckons those in Christ to have died with Him. The law cannot touch a dead man. We have been released from the law so that we can serve in newness of the Spirit, not in "oldness" of the letter. Laws cannot produce life; they only draw lines of right and wrong. Paul argues that if a law had been given that was able to impart life, then righteousness would indeed have been based on the law (Gal. 3:21); but the law is an impotent husband—he cannot impart life.

Now we have died to the law so that we might be married to Christ and bear fruit for God (Rom. 7:4). Jesus is full of life. He is no impotent husband. He wants me to abide in Him and He in me so that I can bear much fruit. A completely different arrangement! He removes my condemnation by actually removing my guilt; then He imparts life through our love relationship so that I can actually bear fruit for God.

The tragedy comes when the new convert, having discovered grace through the gospel, returns to the old husband of law in order to live out his new life. This always leads to bondage and despair. After a period of heaviness of soul, he comes back to Jesus to receive free pardon again and shake off his guilt. But all too often he fails to understand what he is doing and again imposes new laws on himself in order never to fail Jesus again. What a tangle! No wonder many Christians testify to being "up and down." I suggest they are more "husband to husband."

Discharged!

We are discharged from the law. Imagine a soldier who enlists in the Army for an agreed period. During this time he is subjected to all the rigors and discipline of military training. He is under authority. Orders must be obeyed meticulously. But the day comes when his agreed term is completed, and he is discharged. On that very day he strolls carelessly across the parade ground— a free man.

Suddenly, the sergeant turns the corner and sees him. Horrified at the sight of this slovenly soldier, he orders him to return, head up, shoulders back, and stand before him at attention.

At first the ex-soldier cringes at the familiar cry, but then remembers he is discharged. "So long, Sarge," he waves. Let the sergeant become ever so red in the face, let the veins stand out ever so prominently on his neck; it's of no consequence. He cannot command the discharged soldier anymore.

We are discharged from the law.

It is essential for us constantly to recognize our death to law. It is no longer the basis for our relationship with God, and it never will be. We are married to Christ; our fulfillment as Christians is bound up in our love relationship with Him.

All evangelicals know that they can never be justified by the law, but what they often fail to realize is that they cannot be sanctified by it either. The law always condemns. Its real purpose is to bring us to Christ (Gal. 3:24).

The tragedy for many believers is that they get caught in a trap. They reach a crisis when they feel deeply challenged by a word from God concerning their sanctification, and they deplore their recent history. With renewed zeal they determine to do better in the future. But at that very moment they make the error that will lead them to certain failure and distress. At the time when they most need to break the snare, they choose the wrong course: they begin to impose certain laws upon themselves in order to help them reign in life. They perhaps adjust their alarm clock for half an hour earlier. They determine to read the whole Bible in the coming year, and so on. These steps may have real worth in and of themselves, but they do not provide us with the keys to "reigning in life." The mistake is in thinking that in order to reign in life we must *do* something, while the New Testament does not teach that. It says that we reign in life by *receiving* the abundance of grace and the free gift of righteousness (Rom. 5:17).

No condemnation

The problem for many Christians is that they always feel condemned. But the answer to condemnation is never simply to improve our performance. It is to reckon on our position through grace.

God has justified us freely as a gift. Condemnation has to do with guilt, not with feelings or improved performance. If we, through grace, are declared "not guilty" by God then we cannot be condemned. Only the guilty man stands condemned. It is God who justifies, and if God has declared us "not guilty" Satan cannot take us to a higher court. There is none. There is no condemnation for us, not because we have been doing well lately, or because we have set ourselves a new standard, but because we are in Christ Jesus. He has carried our guilt on the cross. The more we come to enjoy that truth, the more we will know how to refuse Satan's constant barrage of accusations aimed at getting us down.

If Satan can get us off our ground in Christ Jesus and on to the ground of our effort, he knows he has us in his grip. We may succeed for a while with New Year resolutions but even before February condemnation looms large all over again. The law always kills in the end.

Not only are we free from law, we are also accounted righteous as a gift. Paul tells us that Adam was a type of Christ (Rom. 5:14). We often think of other Old Testament characters as types of Christ: for instance, David and Moses help us to see aspects of Jesus the King, or Jesus the Shepherd; but how does Adam typify him?

In Adam or in Christ?

Adam is a type of Christ in that when he sinned he did so as head of the human race. He thus made us all sinners. We were "in Adam," and therefore were blighted by his sin and guilt. No amount of human activity could make us righteous and get us out of Adam. Even our righteousness was as filthy rags. Countless acts of kindness clocked up nothing on our account. As Thomas Brooks said, "Till men have faith in Christ their best services are but glorious sins." While still in Adam we remain unrighteous and guilty. We can do nothing to be released.

When we are born again we enter a new family with Jesus as the head. Just as Adam's sin and shame were put on our account and all our endeavors at righteousness could not free us from guilt, so now all Jesus' righteousness is credited to us. We are accepted as righteous in Him. Our shortcomings do not disqualify us; we are not relegated to a middle ground somewhere between Jesus and Adam. We are either in Adam and therefore guilty sinners, or in Christ and therefore righteous. Jesus Christ *is* our righteousness, and He is the same, yesterday, today, and forever, whether we feel spiritually high or low. A real grasp of this truth frees God's people from a constant round of condemnation and heaviness. We are *in* the Beloved (Eph. 1:6). God has a dear Son who delights His heart, and we are in Him.

Isaac had a son, named Esau, in whom he delighted. One day, Isaac's other son, Jacob, "clothed himself" with Esau and drew near to his father. Isaac felt his clothing and smelled his smell. He blessed Jacob "in Esau" (Gen. 27). Jacob "hid in" his big brother as a trick and received his father's blessing; but we have been placed in Christ by a loving Father, who now blesses us for Christ's sake with every spiritual blessing. He is not, like Isaac, alarmed to find us hiding there. He has placed us there and is pleased to bless us for Christ's sake.

Just as some early Christians under Jewish influence were tempted to be circumcised to make sure they were acceptable to God, many modern Christians develop external religious habits to try to be worthy of the grace that God wants to give them freely. The wife of an elder in a church in Washington, D.C. told me she had listened ten times to my tape on the grace of God in order to find freedom from past legalism. In Cape Town, South Africa, a woman approached me at the end of a meeting where I had been handling a similar theme. "Is it really true?" she asked me, with tears pouring down her face. She then told me about her church background. Legalistic practices had completely robbed her of the joy of her salvation. Many, therefore, find themselves taken up with the details of externalism, preoccupied with lists of places to which they should not go, clothes they should not wear, things they should not do.

This in turn tragically affects the gathering of the saints. Preoccupied with the rules and regulations, we find ourselves watching to see if others are keeping them properly, and we fail to discover one another as true friends. When I realize that I am "accepted in the Beloved" I find myself free to receive you who are also accepted. Now we are free to interact on a new basis altogether. Relationships within churches that are seeking restoration have been greatly affected by this truth.

Dangerous doctrine?

Isn't this a dangerous doctrine, to say that Christians are righteous without reference to the law? Aren't we in danger of running riot—of doing whatever we like and still regarding ourselves as righteous? Paul anticipates that bone of contention in Romans 6 when he asks, "Are we to continue in sin that grace might increase?" His reply is unyielding: "By no means!" He then goes on to show that we who have been placed in Christ have been united with Him in His death and burial, and that, having thus died, we are freed from sin.

When Jesus was taken from the cross He was buried in the tomb, burial being the final act declaring death to be past. At conversion we are commanded to be baptized in the name of Jesus, and there our burial takes place—not as an effort to kill the old man, but as a declaration that our old man has died together with Christ. We do not bury people in order to kill them but bury because they have died. We are not told to seek after a "death to sin" experience but to acknowledge that by virtue of being joined to Jesus we are partakers of His death (Rom. 6:4; Col. 2:12). In the New Testament this is as much a statement of fact as is the declaration that two men were crucified with Christ, one on the right and one on the left. We believe that two men were crucified with Christ. We must similarly receive the truth that we were crucified with Him (Gal. 2:20).

I do not remember sinning in Adam in the Garden of Eden, nor do I remember dying on the cross with Christ. However, the Bible states as fact that both have happened (Rom. 5:17-21). Now I am to live in awareness of that fact.

It's true, so reckon on it!

Having established the truth of our death in Christ, Paul goes on with the command that we should therefore reckon it to be true in our daily lives (Rom. 6:11). We do not reckon it as true in order to make it true, but because it *is* true.

I was helped in this matter once when I arrived at an overseas airport to be told that, in that particular country (I think it was Spain), the time was 4 p.m. My own watch told me that it was actually 3 p.m. As an Englishman I now had to pretend that the time was four o'clock, when I knew perfectly well that it was actually one hour earlier. Strangely, I did not find that I had to call up all my willpower to make myself believe that it was 4 o'clock. The truth of the matter was that when I was in Spain, the time was 4 p.m.

So it is with us as we step out of Adam into Christ. I do not have to reckon, concentrating my willpower to believe that I am now dead to sin. The Bible teaches that when you are in Christ you are dead to sin, just as when I was in Spain it was 4 o'clock. Therefore, reckon it to be so!

The gospel sets us free from sin. It is good news indeed. First, it delivers us from condemnation and gives us righteousness. Then it releases us from the power of sin and puts us under the power of righteousness. Having understood our clear ground of victory, as Christians we now live by faith. We fight the good fight of faith.

When Abraham was promised that he would father a son he could have strongly contested it, since all his previous experience argued against that possibility. Instead he became fully convinced that what God had promised He was also able to perform (Rom. 4:21). He grew strong in faith giving glory to God.

When the Scripture promises us freedom from sin we are prone immediately to consider our previous track record and we fail to listen to the life-giving Word. Faith comes from hearing, and hearing by the word of Christ. If God has promised it, He is able to perform it *in* us and *through* us and to write His laws on our hearts, thus freeing us from the power of temptation. The righteous man *shall* live by faith.

Good news, not good advice

Any delay in a full realization of this promise in daily life does not negate the promise any more than the delay in Isaac's birth did. Either the promise is true or it is not. When Abraham fell short in his early experience it did not disqualify him from total fulfillment later. He was restored to the promise. So we too must learn to confess and receive forgiveness for failure, but not to abandon the promised goal of freedom.

Many come to regard failure as inevitable and settle for constant confession as the Christian way. It is essential to let the word of faith work in us, telling us what the truth of the matter really is. We must go on believing until full realization is our experience. Although the Good News Bible translates Romans 6:14 as "sin must not rule over you," happily the gospel is even better news than that: it actually says, "sin shall not be master over you," (see, for example, KJV, RV, RSV, NASB, NIV), "for you are not under law but under grace."

CHAPTER 5

Clothed with Power from on High

When Jesus told the disciples they were going to receive power when the Holy Spirit came upon them (Luke 24:49; Acts 1:8), it would not have been a strange concept to them. As Jews they knew their Old Testament and would remember how the Holy Spirit fell on a number of their ancient heroes.

The Spirit had come upon David and Elisha and other kings and prophets. Then there were the Judges, who were particularly marked out by this powerful endowment. Cowardly Gideon had been transformed into a mighty warrior when the Spirit came upon him.

Later on, Isaiah and particularly Joel had prophesied a coming day of widespread outpouring of the Holy Spirit, and then John the Baptist had introduced Jesus as the one who would not only take away sin but would also baptize in the Holy Spirit.

Throughout His ministry Jesus said comparatively little about the Holy Spirit until in the upper room just before Gethsemane. Now He was preparing to depart from His disciples and was preparing them to receive another like Him. So, on the day of Pentecost, we find in an upper room 120 people who are suddenly filled with the Spirit. We all know the story.

Where do we fit in?

The question that still arises for many Christians is, "Where do we fit into all this?" Are we automatically filled at our conversion or do we have to wait for an endowment of the Spirit, as did the disciples? As a young Christian, I found this a very perplexing question. I read all the books on the subject that I could lay my hands on, and I concluded that if great men of God like John Stott and Dr. Martyn Lloyd-Jones could not agree about it then there was very little hope that I could work it out. I was, however, personally persuaded that I needed power from God. I tried to pray by myself about it and take the experience by faith. For a while I was able to convince myself that something had happened, but gradually it all drained away and I had to admit the depressing truth that I was no different from before.

For me, the whole thing came to a head one Sunday afternoon. I had been leading a Bible study for the young people at our church, and I decided to get some fresh air before the evening service. Mounting my motor scooter, I headed for Brighton, on the English coast, not far from where I lived. In the area known as the Fish Market an embarrassing spectacle met my eyes. Surrounded by a crowd of laughing people and assailed by assorted coins and cigarette packets, two elderly ladies were preaching the gospel. The whole scene with its Bible text banners, the reedy voices of the old ladies, the mockery of the crowd, filled me with shame.

"Why does it have to be like this?" I thought.

"You are ashamed because these are old ladies," came the answer, "and in the Bible I called vigorous young men to do this sort of thing. But these old ladies are willing to do it. Are you?"

"Lord, I would rather die than stand in the open air like that," I honestly replied.

Just then I was aware of two men in front of me who were joining in the general mirth. I overheard one of them say, "Look at those old fools! Why can't they keep their religion to themselves? Why don't they keep it in their churches?"

Again I heard a voice inside me, "If you can't stand up and preach, at least you can own Me to these two men. Tell them you're a Christian."

I recoiled even from this prospect. I could speak to Christians with great confidence, but I had never been able to talk to the unconverted about Jesus. I felt ashamed of my cowardice. Miserable, I went home, then got on my knees and prayed, "O God, I must be filled with the Spirit."

Jesus said, "If any one thirst, let him come to me and drink. He who believes in me, as the scripture has said, 'Out of his heart shall flow rivers of living water'" (John 7:37-38, RSV). God has His ways of making us thirsty. I was parched.

The next day, when I arrived at work in London, I phoned a friend with whom I often had lunch.

"Derek," I said, "I must see you. Can we meet at lunchtime?" He readily agreed.

I knew there was something different about Derek. Often, as we shared a table with others in a cafe, he would talk with them about Christ and give them a tract, while I squirmed. He would talk freely about the Lord. I found it all so embarrassing. I hated his freedom while at the same time longing for it with all my heart.

I told him how I felt; then I said, "I must have what you've got." He invited me to come to his church the following Sunday, saying that someone there would pray for me to be baptized in the Holy Spirit.

The following weekend found me traveling to London to stay with Derek. On Saturday evening I met some of the young people from the chapel; they were going on a bus trip into the country to take part in a meeting at another church. Never had I seen such a zealous, vital group. One after another they stood up and gave their testimonies in that meeting without any prior warning or preparation. This was magnificent. The young people I was used to would need a few weeks' notice for this sort of thing, and even then they would have read from notes.

For the first time in my life I heard someone speak in tongues during the course of a meeting. And then, to my astonishment, one of the young Londoners who had been laughing and joking on the coach earlier gave an interpretation. To my dumbfounded ears it sounded as if someone like Isaiah had come into the room. It was all in a different league from anything I had ever encountered before, but I knew that this was what I needed.

The next afternoon I was taken to a special meeting for those who wanted to be baptized in the Holy Spirit. The previous day Derek had been fasting and praying with me about my need to be filled with the Spirit, and he had spoken a prophecy. I had never heard this gift being used before, but I received it as if God Himself were speaking to me. "My little sheep," He said, "keep very close to Me, and I will lead you to living waters and give you your heart's desire." Having heard that promise, I had no doubt that God was going to fill me with His Spirit.

The pastor moved along the line, praying for each one in turn to be filled with the Spirit. Eventually he came to me and laid his hands on my head.

All my expectations and hopes were shattered. I felt nothing at all.

When the pastor finished praying for me, the people around me said, "Well, praise the Lord, then." Everyone in the room was praising the Lord, except me; but I refused to join in. How could I praise the Lord when nothing had happened?

"I want something real from God," I protested.

I was then shown from the Bible the place of faith in all our dealings with God. I saw that I had done all I could do. I had come to God and must now believe Him. So I turned back to God and quietly said, "Thank you, Lord."

That did not satisfy my friends, however. "Come on, Terry," they encouraged me. "Praise God in tongues." I longed to be able to do just that, but how? "Just begin to speak!" they told me. They reminded me that it was not God who spoke in tongues on the day of Pentecost, but that the disciples themselves spoke with other tongues as the Spirit gave them utterance (Acts 2:4).

It all sounded most unsatisfactory to me, but, in spite of all my arguments, my friends prevailed. I spoke out the sounds that came to my mind. Even as I did so a thousand voices in my mind were mocking me, telling me that I was making it all up. I stopped, but my friends encouraged me to carry on. I did so, battling against the doubts that were flooding my mind.

Through all these doubts, I heard my friend's fiancee speak. "You know, you're very clever, Terry, if you're making all this up. You've been doing it for ages."

There was something about the way she said it that made me laugh, and that laughter broke all the tension of the situation. I realized how worried I had become about it all, how self-defeating it was to get so intense. As I relaxed it was as if a flood of the Spirit went through me. I responded to God in words of praise I would never have used before: "Jesus, I love You. Jesus, You're wonderful. Abba, my Father." Words that I previously would have considered almost effeminate now expressed something that I knew and felt about God: I knew that He had filled me with His Holy Spirit.

It was so glorious to be able to praise God freely that I sat in the very back row of the church that evening, put my hand over my mouth so that no one would be disturbed, and spoke in tongues right through the service. I just could not bring myself to stop!

I was soon to find that my experience would not go uncontested. When I arrived back in my home town that night my sister was waiting for me, wanting to find out what had happened. When I told her that I had been baptized in the Spirit, her response was immediate: "Please pray for me."

With little understanding of how to help someone in such a situation, knowing only what had just happened to me in London, I prayed for her. Because of my ignorance of how to prepare her to believe God, she was disappointed. She cried and cried for God to fill her, but nothing happened.

I was not ready for this sort of thing, and found myself assailed by doubts again. The devil rushed in to suggest that what had happened to me was all right in London; but I was back home now, and I was no different. It was just an experience that had come and gone.

For a week I felt cut off from God. I was in turmoil. Had that experience in London been real or not? There was nobody I could turn to, because at that time I knew nobody in the area who had had this experience of the Spirit. Finally, the next Sunday afternoon, I got down on my knees in my bedroom and cried to God for an answer. As I prayed, my joy came flooding back; I began to praise God in tongues again. He had come to abide with me forever. I was out of the wilderness.

Not "whistling in the dark"

God has impressed on me the need to show inquirers the biblical reasons why we should expect to receive the Holy Spirit, so that when we pray we are not "whistling in the dark" and simply hoping something might happen.

Having shared the doctrine of receiving the Holy Spirit I assure people that the promise is to everyone the Lord calls (Acts 2:39); then I lay hands on them, encouraging them to believe. I have never felt it right to tell people that they have automatically received; nor do I try to force them to speak in tongues, but simply invite them to come and drink in the light of the clear promises of the Lord Jesus and to expect the manifestation of speaking in tongues.

When I saw these principles some six months after my first sad attempt, I again prayed for my sister and had the joy of seeing her and her roommate immediately receive the Holy Spirit.

Within weeks, others of my friends began to receive the Spirit, and very soon we found ourselves on that same Brighton seafront, standing on boxes and preaching the gospel. I began to go from door to door, telling people about Jesus. I went into coffee bars wherever I could see groups of young people with whom I could share the Lord. All these things had been utterly impossible to me before, but now I had a glorious new freedom to proclaim Christ.

There is a teaching that claims that every believer automatically receives the power of the Holy Spirit at conversion. It seems to me that this claim does not stand up under investigation of the Scriptures. The new converts at Samaria, in giving their testimony, would have said that they were converted through the preaching of Philip the evangelist, and that a few days later they received the power of the Holy Spirit when Peter and John laid hands upon them (Acts 8:5-17). Similarly, it was three days after Paul's Damascus Road conversion that he received the Holy Spirit through the laying on of Ananias' hands (Acts 9:17). Likewise, the apostle Paul told the Ephesian disciples about Christ; then, subsequent to their baptism he laid hands upon them, whereupon they received the Holy Spirit and spoke in tongues (Acts 19:6). For them both experiences took place on the same day, but they can still be seen as two separate experiences.

Why "tarry"?

Some have taught that people should "tarry" until they receive the Holy Spirit and speak in tongues, but I believe this displays an undue concentration on the day of Pentecost and a disregard of other accounts in the Book of Acts.

After Pentecost no one was ever told to wait for the Holy Spirit. Peter and John immediately laid hands on the Samaritan converts. Ananias did not tell Paul to find a place to wait for the Spirit; he immediately laid hands on the three-day-old believer. Paul, having led the Ephesians to Christ and having baptized them in water, did not hesitate to lay hands on them for the baptism of the Holy Spirit.

During His ministry on earth, Jesus said the Spirit was not yet given, not because people hadn't waited long enough or weren't ready yet, but because He was not yet glorified (John 7:39). Once He was glorified this truth was proclaimed on the day of Pentecost. No one was ever again told to wait for the endowment of power.

Come and drink!

The stage is now set for anyone who thirsts to delay no longer, but to come to Him and drink; to look not at their own shortcomings but to God's Word: the promise is to everyone whom the Lord our God shall call. The laying on of hands is clearly biblical, and I thank God for those who so lovingly and patiently prayed with me.

It is increasingly our practice to first bring people to faith in the Lord Jesus Christ, and then, very soon after, to lay hands upon them to receive the power of the Holy Spirit.

Some Christians mistakenly believe that receiving the baptism of the Holy Spirit is for mature believers, those who have walked with God for a long time and are now qualified to receive. But again, Scripture shows us clearly that new converts received it. The promise is to "all that the Lord our God shall call." Evidently, God considers it essential that Christians receive power from on high as soon as possible after their new birth in order to live a life that is full of "righteousness, peace and joy in the Holy Spirit." The baptism of the Holy Spirit is not a reward for doing so well on our own. It is a gift to enable you to overcome right from the start.

Some years ago at a meeting in Brighton I led a young lady to the Lord. The following week she came to my home to see me about being filled with the Spirit. She brought along her apartment-mate, who was also full of questions, prompted by the dramatic change in her friend's life. I happened to be out, but my wife led the second girl to the Lord. When I came home I found the two new Christians, one a week old in Christ, the other about twenty minutes. I counseled them, laid hands on both of them, and had the joy of seeing both receive the baptism of the Holy Spirit and joyfully praising God in new tongues.

Such stories could multiply again and again as crowds of new converts receive the power of the Holy Spirit.

Of course, there is great danger in regarding this as a once-and-for-all experience. Many have only the memory of a date when they initially received the Spirit—perhaps many years ago.

The early believers were mistaken for drunks. To remain drunk, one must keep drinking! In early Acts we see the apostles not only filled on the day of Pentecost but filled again and again. I thank God that my initial and glorious experience in London has been followed by fresh fillings of the Spirit, several of which have surpassed the first in terms of the enjoyment of the glory of God.

I believe God is teaching us new things about the need for fresh fillings of His Spirit that deliver us from undue glorying in the past. We must avoid the trap some have fallen into: after a prolonged time of hungering and thirsting for God they receive the Holy Spirit, only to go on to a time of spiritual decline because they regard themselves as having "arrived" through their initial experience.

As that mighty pioneer, Smith Wigglesworth, is recorded as saying:

> I would rather have a man on my platform not filled with the Holy Ghost but hungry for God than a man that has received the Holy Ghost but has become satisfied with his experience.[1]

An even sadder mistake is to miss the experience altogether, failing to enter into the inheritance that God has provided for us. As Dr. Martyn Lloyd-Jones said:

> The great and constant danger is that we should be content with something that is altogether less than that intended for us . . . . In other words, certain people by nature are afraid of the supernatural, of the unusual, of disorder. You can be so afraid of disorder, so concerned about discipline and decorum and control, that you become guilty of what the scripture calls "quenching the Spirit" and there is no question in my mind that there has been a great deal of this.[2]

Happily in these days thousands are abandoning that old cautious stance and are pressing in to their inheritance, receiving the promise of the Father.

But what sort of church is needed for people so filled with joy and praise? Certainly one that is open to a release of worship in the Spirit.

CHAPTER 6

Worship in Spirit and Truth

"Would you please come and be our first full-time pastor?" The invitation came from a new church getting started in Seaford, on the south coast of England. I had just completed my three years at London Bible College, and said that I was very open to the invitation—providing they were open to the baptism of the Holy Spirit, as well as Spirit-led worship and congregational participation (usually known as "body ministry").

It seemed essential to me to be open and straightforward about my objectives for a local church. I was no stranger to the little fellowship. They said they trusted me to be biblical and balanced; they had heard me preach on receiving the Holy Spirit, among other things, and were happy to proceed on that basis.

I was determined not to settle for the "one-man ministry" and the "hymn-sandwich" type of service, with a passive congregation simply coming to listen to the sermon. I was looking for a dynamic, Spirit-filled worship meeting full of the presence of the Lord.

At first we introduced a ten-minute time of open prayer and praise into the conventional four-hymn program. This gradually became twenty minutes, then half an hour, and eventually more like an hour.

Open worship

It was not smooth sailing, however, as any pastor might guess.
Some were very uneasy about this new idea. I well remember one
of the first meetings. One of the elders of the church, a large, no-
nonsense man who was very uneasy about these experiments,
sat opposite me. I explained to the church the concept of "open
worship" and waited in the increasingly oppressive silence. After
the pause, one of the elderly ladies, grasping the idea that we
could now sing "choruses" in our morning worship, searched her
childhood memories and asked if we could now sing "A little talk
with Jesus makes it right, all right." My heart sank. My co-elder's
head sank into his hands. As the weeks went by I had to explain
that worship did not consist of singing songs for "those in peril
on the sea," just because that may be a favorite old hymn.

Gradually people were receiving the Holy Spirit, and the tide
was coming in—but why do the irresponsible ones have to
receive first? The morning meetings became an agony before
ultimately becoming an ecstasy. Some seemed totally unaware of
how others were struggling to cope with the changes and would
suddenly speak in tongues with great abandonment. As pastor,
I had to clear up the mess: correction here, explanation there;
more teaching from the Bible on love and patience and forbearance. At last we began to experience the sort of meetings of which
I had dreamed. An hour of worship became a glorious time in the
presence of God. People were increasingly sensitive to one
another and to the Lord, who was manifestly among us.

The true circumcision

In New Testament times, there were many who claimed to be the
true people of God. Paul had to show how the true church of his
day could be identified. He gave a description that is both
revealing and challenging. He said, "We are the true circumcision
[that is, the real people of God], who worship in the Spirit of God
and glory in Christ Jesus and put no confidence in the flesh" (Phil.

3:3). We would have expected him to identify them by referring to a certain doctrinal formula, or perhaps association with the early apostles. How strange that the first characteristic he lists is worship in the Spirit.

"Worship," said A.W. Tozer, "is the missing jewel in the evangelical church."[1] Yet Paul sees it as the hallmark signifying the true people of God. The radical church, in seeking its true roots, must give high priority to the place of worship. How many of us have been raised on the meager diet of three hymns before and one after the minister's sermon? This is seen as normal fare in evangelical circles, but how far removed from the biblical norm. Jesus tells us that God is seeking those who will worship Him in Spirit and truth. We are called to be, among other things, a holy priesthood offering up spiritual sacrifices acceptable to God (1 Pet. 2:5). Can this dull routine that masquerades as a time of worship really be satisfying His heart? Nor do I mean that we simply introduce a few guitars and scripture songs, or that we simply be permitted to raise and clap our hands and get emotional.

I well remember the agonies of our first experiences of hand raising and clapping in the meetings. It somehow seemed a shocking thing to do in church. There were very painful battles to be fought, but now I thank God that we enjoy the fruits of victories won. Now we enjoy increasingly beautiful orchestras in our churches, with violins and cellos, trumpets and cymbals, all reminding us of the great majesty of God and helping to bring worship that is more in keeping with His glory. Somehow the old harmonium said nothing to us of the glory of God, whereas the crashing cymbals—skillfully played—certainly do.

Praise Him with understanding

True worship must involve our whole being. Mind, heart, and will must harmonize to magnify God's name. We must praise Him with understanding so that we will not encourage mindless ditties. Nor shall we battle with ancient language hardly understood by a generation fast approaching the twenty-first century. Exhortations to "try to lift the roof off this time" have more to do with NCAA conference finals than with worship, and to be told to "sing it as though you really mean it" is sacrilege. What is the difference between that and an outright invitation to be hypocrites? If any worship leader feels he has to make such a request then everyone has already missed the point of worshiping in truth. A careless mental attitude prevents true worship.

It is because we take things seriously that we consider to whom we are singing. "Stand up and bless the Lord" is not sung to God but to one another, and so should be truly addressed to our brothers and sisters. On the other hand, idly gazing around while singing "Within the Veil" betrays a mind wandering rather than worshiping. Nor am I advocating individuals rejoicing in their newly found liberty by simply choosing their favorites. The question is, "What do I want to say to God and what would be appropriate in the Spirit at this time in the meeting?" In that attitude of mind we must find the song of worship most suitable for the moment.

The doctrinal content of our songs of worship will determine to a greater or lesser degree their real spiritual value. That is why scriptures set to music are so edifying. It's not enough that the melody is sweet and the lyric sentimental. What an anticlimax to find that when we sing "kings and kingdoms shall all pass away," we only add, "but there's something about that name." What do we mean? What are we singing?

A time of worship is a fresh opportunity to get to know God. We can grow in faith as we declare glorious truths about Him and to Him. Often there will be a freedom coming from Him as we touch His holiness and experience His love melting our hearts afresh.

"Worship is pure or base as the worshiper entertains high or low thoughts of God."[2] It is the truth that sets us free, and truth sung with faith and in the power of the Spirit can have a mighty, liberating effect upon us. It sometimes takes time to develop from praise into heartfelt adoration. Our hearts need to be tuned into

God's presence and power. Worship must be in spirit as well as in truth, and we should expect our emotions to be roused.

Make a joyful noise

Many have dismissed a joyful, liberated expression of worship as mere emotionalism, but C. H. Spurgeon said, "I would sooner risk the dangers of a tornado of religious excitement than see the air grow stagnant with a dead formality."[3] Of course emotion will be released—God has commanded it! We are told to rejoice before Him, clap our hands, shout and sing.

The meetings that our reserved, English, conservative culture has produced are far removed from the Jewish roots of our heritage. In the name of reverence many have banned clapping or raising of hands from their churches. These are replaced by the whispering associated with the library or museum. But true reverence has to do with obedience, and God has commanded us to worship Him wholeheartedly. Let us reverently obey Him!

We are told that David and all the house of Israel were celebrating before the Lord with all kinds of instruments as they brought the ark to Jerusalem. Suddenly, God struck a man dead for touching the ark. He was judged for his presumption. However, having replaced the cart by the correct God-appointed ark-bearers, David did not walk sedately to express his reverence, but even after that fearful manifestation of God's holiness he danced before the Lord with all his might (2 Sam. 6).

Some have argued that Old Testament worship was external, with its clapping, dancing, and use of instruments, whereas New Testament worship is internal because it is in spirit and in truth. However, we have often been left with something that is neither spiritual nor truthful. The New Testament says, "You greatly rejoice with joy inexpressible and full of glory" (1 Pet. 1:8). Many evangelicals are in danger of joining forces with liberals, selecting verses here and explaining away verses there. The liberal's assertion, "It doesn't mean He really multiplied the five loaves" is not so different from, "Of course it doesn't mean real indescribable joy."

Some modern theologians teach that the wedding guests at Cana did not actually taste miraculously provided new wine. It is sad to see many a good man arguing for the reality of new wine in Cana, but failing to lead his congregation into the "new wine" that Jesus is providing today.

Captives return singing

Surely our inability to express true joy in worship in the past has been at least partly due to our spiritual bondage. "How can we sing the Lord's song in a foreign land?" asked the captive psalmist when his tormentors demanded one of the songs of Zion (Ps. 137:4). However, Psalm 126 tells a different story:

> When the Lord brought back the captive ones of Zion, we were like those who dream. Then our mouth was filled with laughter, and our tongue with joyful shouting (Ps. 126:1-2).

The psalmist who could not sing while in captivity could hardly stop singing when delivered! Tragically, traditions that bind rather than loose have developed in church life during the cold years of spiritual bondage. Established church services leave very little room for true delight in God. Any who claim that their genuine authority is the Bible, not church tradition, must by God's grace make adjustments to obey His Word (Matt. 15:6).

It has even been suggested that God developed the denominations with their different styles of worship in order that we could select the one that reflects our own preference and temperament. All extroverts can join the Pentecostals, while more sober believers can settle elsewhere. What a tragic misunderstanding of God's purpose.

God is seeking those who will worship Him "in spirit and truth," not "in temperament and preference." In God's glorious kingdom extroverts will learn to be hushed in awe before Him and those formerly inhibited will be drunk with new wine. Peter did not argue on the day of Pentecost, "These are not all drunk as you suppose but are a group of extroverts who prefer this kind of worship." Certainly there will be great diversity in times of worship; the variety, though, should be not a reflection of our human failings and limitations but an outshining of the glorious multifaceted grace of God.

The house of God should also be the gate of heaven (Gen. 28:17). God wants His house rebuilt that He might take pleasure in it and appear in His glory. It is, therefore, to be a place of encounter with God where the unbeliever coming in will fall on his face and worship God, declaring that He is certainly among you (1 Cor. 14:25). Radical surgery is called for in local church life to make room for such encounters.

It is not enough for us to keep our traditional Sunday meetings as they have always been while we slip away to a mid-week charismatic house group in order to praise the Lord. What is our justification for retaining the unbiblical meeting? The Holy Spirit wants to lead us into greater heights and depths of praise. The New Testament spiritual house made of living stones must outshine the Old Testament temple. There they prophesied with lyres and harps and cymbals, but that was just the dispensation of death.

A better covenant

Paul argues that if the old covenant of death and condemnation was glorious, how much more will the new covenant of the Spirit and righteousness abound in glory (2 Cor. 3:9-11). The bright moon may dominate the dark night sky, but it is barely visible by day when the sun's glory fills the heavens.

Prophetic songs accompanied by Spirit-gifted musicians were present in the Old Testament. Many of us are now enjoying meetings like this every Sunday, but we want to know more. We feel like Moses, who cried to God, "You have only begun to show Your servant Your greatness." On some occasions when we sing in the Spirit together and Spirit-inspired songs and visions are shared, we can say with Jacob, "This is the house of God, this is the gate of heaven." Gone are the days when worship was seen merely as the preliminary before the all-important sermon.

We are a royal priesthood, all wanting to bring our Spirit-inspired contribution to fulfill our calling as a priesthood of all believers. The radical church must shake off the shackles of timid and drab conservatism. In looking for our true biblical roots, let us joyfully unearth the atmosphere of the New Testament church. As Dr. Martyn Lloyd-Jones has put it:

> Here is a gathering of men and women who are filled with the Spirit of God, and each one of them has got something; one a psalm, one a doctrine, one a revelation, one an interpretation, one a tongue. When one gave his contribution the others rejoiced and they praised God together; and they were all in a state of great joy and glory and happiness.

> Our danger is that we tend to judge and to think of the New Testament meetings with what we are familiar with in our deadness. Here is joy, here is inspiration, here is illumination, here is something that is given by the power and the work of the Spirit. There is so much life and power that the Apostle has to say, "Now you have got to control this. Let everything be done decently and in order." There were excesses in the church at Corinth, but what does Paul say to them? Does he say, "Never speak in tongues again, never prophesy again, never give vent to these feelings that you have within you"? He does not say anything of the sort. The whole atmosphere in the early church was charged with the Spirit and they expressed that in psalms and hymns and spiritual songs.

> The really important question for us to face is, are we like the early church, are we like the early Christians, rejoicing and praising God, filled with gladness and joy so that we amaze the world and make them think at times that we are filled with new wine? Let us avoid all excesses, let everything be done decently and in order, but above all quench not the Spirit. Rather be filled with the Spirit and give evidence of the fact that you are.[4]

It is the ultimate scandal that people ignore the church because she is so boring. Her meetings are so predictable and gray. God has made a world of magnificent color and variety, but it is only a garment that ultimately will be discarded. Though they have such a fleeting existence, God does not make two snowflakes alike. But the glorious church will live forever, a bride adorned for her husband. She is the pinnacle of God's creative skill, destined to show forth the multicolored wisdom of God (see Eph. 3:10). How she needs to arise, shine, and put on her beautiful garments of praise and worship in spirit and truth.

"It's a pity the church isn't like this"

When we recently rented a vacation camp for a teens and twenties week, the employees of the camp were amazed at the life and joy expressed in our praise and worship. "It's a pity the church isn't like this," they said. We were able to tell them of a number of churches that were very much like that! The unconverted could see the need for new wineskins to contain the life of these young people who were thrilled and filled with God.

Another group booked 200 places at a camp. Hundreds of non-Christians filled two adjoining halls—one being used for a disco, the other for a boxing match. The manager expressed his concern for us when he asked, "What about the noise?" We replied that *they* would have to put up with it! They not only put up with it but pressed their faces against the windows of our meeting hall to witness the life there.

One Sunday, about 400 praised God and sang and danced on Brighton seafront. They could be heard from quite a distance away. Many stopped to listen and take literature. On arriving a little late, I parked my car in a nearby street. A couple passed me, wanting to discover what the joyful scene was about. "It sounds as though the pubs have turned out," they said.

It was not an enemy of the church who recorded that the first meeting looked like a crowd of drunks. Luke seemed neither embarrassed nor ashamed of the seemingly insulting comparison. We are exhorted not to be drunk with wine but to be filled with the Spirit (Eph. 5:18). There are real comparisons as well as contrasts between being full of the Holy Spirit and full of new wine, and the Bible draws that to our attention more than once.

Not only should we as individuals know the new wine of the Spirit, but our church life must be sufficiently flexible to cope with the joyful exuberance that such "drunkenness" brings. New wine in new wineskins. New songs from new creatures enjoying a new covenant. God can deliver us from staleness at any point. He makes all things new.

CHAPTER 7

Making Friends

hen I was converted I lost all my friends. As teenagers we had grown up together; we enjoyed marvelous experiences and our friendship was very real. Late into the night we would talk about our innermost hopes and fears. It broke my heart when none of my friends wanted to come with me into my newly found Christian life. I often wept for them in prayer. After a while, I began to weep for myself. I was so lonely. It was wonderful to know my sins were forgiven and that I was going to heaven, but life was miserable in the here and now.

On Sundays I was inspired by the minister's wonderful preaching, but I was lost in the crowd and nobody seemed to notice me. Gradually, as time slipped by, I grew in experience and found that this was true for so many. Formal acquaintance seemed to be the standard in the church. People who had known one another for years were still on handshake and surname terms. Real friendship such as I had grown up with and so valued was almost entirely missing. After a couple of years I was received into membership and given "the right hand of fellowship." But nothing changed.

Abundant meetings!

The Christian life therefore seemed to be a matter of losing all my old ungodly friends and in their place simply attending meetings.

In the agony of my loneliness I threw myself into every meeting available. My week included Sunday morning and evening services, Monday prayer meeting, Tuesday youth fellowship, Wednesday Bible School, Thursday male voice choir (I had to go somewhere!), Friday Boys' Brigade, and Saturday prayer meeting. But in all this—no friends!

When people began to meet in homes, sharing their newly found charismatic experience, they started finding natural friendship again. The very informality of the living room was so different from always meeting in the church building on its hard, upright pews or chairs.

First names replaced surnames and, unexpectedly, Russian-style hugs replaced handshakes. Intimate prayer fellowship, where God's presence was felt, also melted cold formality. Drunkenness through alcohol, which often released and seemingly enriched my old friendships, was replaced by a new Holy Spirit drunkenness that led to laughter, joy, and freedom among Christians. New experiences drew us out of our shells: the first stumbling attempts at speaking in tongues and interpretation or prophecy, gathering around individuals in need to lay hands on them and pray. All these experiences helped to knit people in friendship.

For some, the leap to real friendship proves so difficult that something else creeps in. Instead of genuine friendship comes a strange super-spirituality: syrupy-sweet choruses followed by obscure readings or visions, shared in an atmosphere of growing unreality.

A new experience of the Spirit opens the way to the possibility of friendship, but it does not guarantee it. We do not automatically make friends by meeting in charismatic prayer meetings instead of in formal church services. True friendship calls for open-eyed confrontation as well as melting moments of worship.

Openness

True friendship has to be developed outside of Christian meetings. For friendship to flourish there must be openness, honesty, and loyalty. We must be willing to come out from behind our masks and religious jargon and get to know each other openly.

As a local pastor, when I first introduced house groups I invited people to bring board games such as Scrabble and Monopoly, not in order to discover their expertise with words or property purchase, but rather to encourage friendship and relaxed relationships. Some were offended, but soon everybody came to see the value of relaxed friendship from which we could build something of genuine worth. As has been said, "A congregation which does not eat hot dogs in real fellowship is not able to celebrate the Lord's supper in the right way."[1] Gradually, open relationships began to replace formal ones, and it was not long before prayer fellowship could tackle not only church issues but personal issues.

But of course lasting, valuable friendships are not superficial. They are frequently challenged by times of misunderstanding, thoughtlessness, and plain sinfulness. How do we cope with the pressures? We try to work out a loyalty based on the commitment required of new covenant people. We are not casual friends; we are blood brothers and sisters in covenant with God and each other. I do not mean a secret, exclusive covenant, limited to a certain framework of elite believers. Jesus commands us to be committed to loving our enemies and opponents. Certainly, then, He expects us to love all our Christian brothers and sisters. John's first letter is full of exhortations to prove our faith by our love for the brethren.

Local churches must become churches where true friendships are formed and a framework is built for their outworking. New converts called out of a former way of life must find that they are called not simply to attend meetings, even charismatic ones. They are brought into a family; they are part of a living community.

Externalism kills friendship

If a congregation is still within the pressures of evangelical legalism and bondage to externalism, true friendship will hardly ever take place. The terrible temptation to put on a front, or to justify one's existence by outward form, quenches the flame of natural warmth and affection. Our attitude to meetings must be like Jesus' attitude to the Sabbath: meetings were made for man, not man for meetings (Mark 2:27). Every service must come under close scrutiny. Is it purposeful? Why do we have it? Is it bearing fruit? What happens as a result of it?

I was once told about a child who asked her mother why she invariably cut off each end of the Sunday roast and placed the pieces on top of the main part before cooking it. Her mother was not sure why she had always done so; she was simply aware that her mother had done it before her. So she got in touch with her own elderly mother and asked her why she had always performed this particular piece of surgery, supposing it allowed the meat juices to flow more freely. She was staggered at the reply. Grandma explained that she had always prepared the roast in that way because her oven had been so small that it was the only way she could get a family-size roast into it!

Many a church meeting has as much relevance to the next generation as this inherited and now totally unnecessary custom. When such dead meetings and religious observances become part of our church life they militate against real friendship, because they militate against reality itself. Upon entering the very church building some people seem to change into other people. Natural speech becomes inappropriate. Normal ways of greeting one another disappear. People start tiptoeing and whispering. Is it any wonder that we have difficulty with warm friendships?

This whole approach is based on a totally wrong doctrine of the church building as the house of God. Evangelical believers know that the church is the people, not the building. We are God's house. Why, then, are we not totally consistent with our doctrine? Some seem to think that the building itself is holy, and even that one end of it is more holy than the other!

At home together

What a contrast we find in the New Testament, where disciples are reclining at the table with Jesus and even leaning on one another. What an atmosphere there must have been when those men were together. What laughter! What joy! What seriousness! What zeal! What excitement! What fun! What friendship!

I thank God for the red-hot zeal for Christ that I find in my friends, and I thank God for the times of riotous laughter we enjoy together as well as the days of prayer and fasting. God has called us to be friends. Jesus called His disciples "friends"; Abraham, as well, was the friend of God. It is difficult to say anything more profound than that.

It is because we feel ourselves to be friends of God that we are freed to be friends with one another. When our relationship with God is based on law (Old Testament or evangelical) we find it very difficult to relax together. We are commanded to receive one another as Christ received us. When I know that God has received you and me just as we are, "warts and all," I can receive you similarly. Neither of us has to pretend. Because of our genuine friendship we can actually help one another in reality. We can honestly share our hopes and fears, failures and frustrations, prayers and longings.

We will only arrive at the maturity God has planned for us as we encourage, exhort, and admonish each other. The New Testament is full of commandments telling us to do a variety of things for one another. We can only obey these commands and discover their power when we get close enough to handle the discomfort and pain of such encounters.

Friendly wounds

When I am assured of my brother's love and genuine friendship, I can receive correction that would be wounding from a comparative stranger. I can even come out of my shell and begin to do some admonishing myself when I know my relationship is secure. We would do well to study all the "one another" verses in the New Testament and ask ourselves how many of them are being obeyed in our local congregation and in our individual lives.

Confrontation can be very difficult, and many avoid it. But what wasted time could be redeemed in our lives if faithful friends started telling us some truths about ourselves. Only a good friend will bother to tell you that you always dominate conversations, that you never listen to anyone else, that you are inconsiderate to your wife, that you are too soft on your children, that you put people off because your breath smells or you don't use deodorant.

Is this the kingdom of God, you may ask? Is it down to such pathetic details? Yes. It is the stuff of life. When Jesus came to save us it was not simply to teach us how to sing hymns and go up and down on our toes at the right time while singing "And Can It Be," or even to raise our hands and dance in worship. It pleases God when we learn to live securely in good relationships, when frightened, lonely people are helped to find true friends and can start enjoying life instead of hiding behind outward forms. People who have been freed from loneliness and introspection make good friends of others, even of the unconverted. Yes—they become natural evangelists.

Large congregations do not provide the setting in which close and intimate friendships thrive. The small house groups which we have been led to make use of are far more helpful to that end.

House group life indispensable

As John Stott argued in his very helpful book, *One People:*

> There is always something unnatural and sub-human about
> large crowds. They tend to be aggregations rather than
> congregations—aggregations of unrelated persons. The larger
> they become the less the individuals who compose them
> know and care about each other. Indeed, crowds can actually
> perpetuate aloneness instead of curing it. There is a need,
> therefore, for large congregations to be divided into smaller
> groups such as one imagines the house churches were in
> New Testament days. The value of the small group is that it
> can become a community of related persons and in it the
> benefit of personal relatedness cannot be missed, nor its
> challenge evaded.[2]

He points out that bars flourish, not because most people are
alcoholics, but because God has put into the human heart the
desire to know and be known and to love and be loved, so that
many seek a counterfeit fellowship at the price of a few beers. He
goes on:

> I do not think it is an exaggeration to say, therefore, that small
> groups, Christian family or fellowship groups, are indispen-
> sable for our growth into spiritual maturity.[3]

The house groups into which churches are being divided are not
simply Bible study groups or prayer groups, though evenings
may often be devoted to either of those vital exercises. Nor is their
purpose to produce a miniature version of the large Sunday
congregational meeting. Whole evenings have often been given
to outdoor picnics, house decoration, evangelism, or church
cleaning.

Caring community

Within the house group everyone has a caring ministry. A vivid demonstration of the sort of relationships we are building occurred when one of the couples in the church experienced a saucepan fire, which destroyed their stove, ruined the kitchen, and badly spoiled the hall and stairway of the house. Before nightfall this particular house boasted a new stove, as well as a repainted and redecorated kitchen, hall, and staircase (the elders did not dictate the decor!).

While another young man was working for his firm in the U.S. for some weeks, his house was almost entirely redecorated by his house-group friends. Such stories abound.

House groups provide a flexible, intimate setting that can be easily subdivided for growth. They prove an ideal setting for evangelism; and, whereas we often find 10 percent outsiders attending our central evangelistic meetings, informal gospel home-group evenings can attract up to 50 percent unconverted.

The house-group leader and his wife play key roles, providing not only a warm, hospitable atmosphere but also helping the elders in the ministry of discipling. They have the care of the group, and, under the elders' supervision, they watch over the little flock in their charge. As they accumulate experience they can be given more responsibility for the people, and so men can begin to display their potential for possible future eldership.

These men are particularly asked to watch out for and encourage new, emerging leaders. Thus the pattern for growth develops. House-group leaders are in constant contact with their elders, both in regular training and fellowship gatherings, and also individually. So the burden of responsibility for leadership of the local church is broadened, and more people find their place of service in the body of Christ.

Jethro's advice

God originally spoke to me on this theme through the advice Jethro gave Moses in Exodus 18:21. I was, at that time, pastoring a growing church, and was regularly preaching twice each Sunday and once mid-week. Jethro's advice to Moses to choose men to share the load proved as revolutionary in my life as it did in Moses'. I chose some able and faithful men: able, or nothing is accomplished; faithful, or they divide the church and destroy the work.

At first, some resented the pastor's absence at the mid-week meetings, or felt that a hospital visit from a house-group leader was not a proper visit but, gradually, changes of attitude came about. One lady complained to me that I had not visited her when she was ill. She reluctantly conceded, however, that several from her house-group had called, whereas formerly only I had fulfilled my pastoral duty. Little by little her values altered, and now she rejoices in the fruits of change in that particular church. She has, herself, become one of the closest of friends and busiest of workers within the family.

We discover our place by accepting one another and serving one another in love, not by being preoccupied with a constant search to identify "our ministry." As we offer our service we are appreciated, thanked, encouraged and corrected and thereby trained. Gradually, we find our particular place. Correction is not to be seen as an outrageous and impertinent invasion into our personal life but a natural part of family relationships. It should not be reserved for encounters of crisis proportions. Disciples are like apprentices: always looking for improvement and open to adjustment.

Paul says to the Roman church, "you yourselves are full of goodness, filled with all knowledge, and able also to admonish one another" (Rom. 15:14). We all have blind spots, and our Christian friends can help us change by speaking plainly.

Happy families

We are deeply grateful for the new emphasis on family life being recovered in the church and have benefited enormously from the ministry of such men as James Dobson. We encourage men to take a responsible attitude toward their families as head of the home, and to raise their children sensitively "in the discipline and instruction of the Lord" (Eph. 6:4).

Although Sunday schools are found in our ranks, most would want to emphasize that they merely provide backup to the parental responsibility of teaching. We have abandoned the idea of aiming our evangelism at the children of the unconverted in order eventually to win the adults. We would much rather reach responsible adults, believing they will bring their own children.

Seminars at our Bible Weeks regularly stress the importance of family life; many local churches have their own teaching programs. We have a strong conviction that Christian family life can speak volumes in our crumbling society to many whose families are in sad disarray. We have to recover a sense of parental involvement in a day when, according to Larry Christenson, drop-out parents can be blamed for much of today's juvenile delinquency.[4]

Views on child-raising vary enormously, but Christians are privileged to know God's view. The father, as head of the family, is responsible for the state of his household. He must therefore be aroused from the apathy associated with modern-day fathers in order to fulfil his God-given role. This also involves the recovery of the biblical order of relationships between husband and wife, abandoned by modern society, and, sadly, by many in the church.

When the Israelites entered Canaan, God had already given them wonderful laws and principles that would make them stand out as a testimony to the nations. The greatest danger they faced was that of disobeying the Lord by worshiping the gods of the land and by imitating the local people's horrific practices, which included child sacrifice.

Today's gods are humanism and liberal thinking, worshiped by many at a terrible cost. Our neighbors may laugh at the standards of the Bible, but they are apparently willing to pay the price of their worship by sacrificing their marriages and producing insecure and troubled children. As Bible-believing Christians, we must be true to what God has shown us and demonstrate to the world how family life is really meant to be enjoyed.

People who get married expect to live alone no longer. But Jesus showed how even people living under the same roof can be living alone. He said that unless a grain of wheat falls into the ground and dies, it remains alone. The only way to be freed from "living alone" is to die to your self-interest. In that sense, a wedding ceremony is also a burial service. Two former individuals die in order to become something else. Something new is being created; they become one flesh.

To enable that marriage partnership to function properly there is a God-given order. It is not a case of "anything goes." The Christian home should be an expression of God's kingdom; therefore, it has divine order.

Husbands and wives

A loving and mutually respectful attitude between husband and wife is the key to good family life. When children see their father loving, protecting, and honoring his wife and giving her her true place in the home, they will learn to respect her themselves.

Larry Christenson writes:

> The highest duty of the Christian husband is to care for the sanctification of his wife. Even the regular pastor of the family must be on his guard against taking upon himself that oversight and care of the spiritual health of the wife which belongs to the husband. If he intrudes into it the husband has the right to repel him. He should leave to the husband the share of the responsibility which rests upon him for the spiritual health of all the members of the family.[5]

When a wife shows true heart submission to her husband, honoring the dignity he has been given as God's appointed head of the house, she demonstrates the way of obedience, which the children can follow.

The right relationship between men and women in the home overflows into our corporate church life. People have often observed a preponderance of men in restoration churches. We live in days when many men of the world have rejected the church as being for women and children. They are therefore often surprised by what they find in our ranks. Men are not only present but are obviously involved in the life of the church.

When I introduced the concept of "open worship" in my first church I was saddened by the immediate predominance of the women in prayer and praise. I had no desire to stop them, feeling that the Bible gives women freedom to pray or prophesy (1 Cor. 11:5), but I longed for the men to be at least as voluble.

I wondered why the ladies were more free to take part. Were the men lazy? Fearful? Self-conscious? Or simply lacking in the kind of fellowship that the women often enjoyed during the daytime? Certainly, many of the women knew each other more intimately and often had daytime prayer fellowship.

Men's meetings

I decided to introduce an occasional men's evening. It was an unstructured time for fellowship, praise, and prayer, and it proved to be an extraordinary turning point in the church's life. The men began to be friends, enjoying amazing times of praise and prophecy as well as laughter and enjoyment. The Sunday meetings were gradually influenced; male/female contributions became balanced.

Later, when I moved to Brighton, we again started a men's meeting. At first it was held in a home with fewer than twenty present. We used the same unstructured style with great success, forming intimate friendships and enjoying wonderful times in the presence of God. Our most recent men's evening was attended by 300 men and was a memorable occasion.

Our area leaders' days are also for men only, and in the last twelve months about 1,000 leaders have gathered for day conferences in which we are involved. One could easily be misunderstood in making this point, but the truth is that there is a certain "something" in getting men together who mean business for God. We have noticed what a profound impact lively men's meetings have on those recently converted. Many have their previous concept of the church completely shattered in one evening. At the risk of sounding simplistic, we do encourage our men to be men!

The women are still very evident and fulfilled in our church life. They take part freely in worship meetings through prayer, prophecy, healing, speaking in tongues, interpretation, singing, Scripture reading, testifying, and, indeed, in every area except where the Bible plainly forbids them. They are therefore not permitted "to teach or exercise authority over a man" (1 Tim. 2:12). Behind the scenes women also play as vital a role in church life as the men. (For a fuller treatment of the role ladies can fulfill in today's church see *Leading Ladies* by Wendy Virgo [Kingsway, 1985]).

Within a family setting, true fathers emerge: people whose counsel you really learn to value. They are not imposed from headquarters, but instead emerge from our ranks. The flock of God finds its shepherds with the anointing and gifting of God so that the whole flock becomes secure.

CHAPTER 8

Flocks and Shepherds

*I*n the ancient world Israel enjoyed a unique privilege. God had spoken to them. They were custodians of the oracles of God—a solemn responsibility, for their progress became dependent on their obedience to the words God had spoken. Disobedience resulted in punishment and captivity. Times of revival were marked by rediscovery of the book of God and fresh obedience to its teaching.

One of the vital keys to restoration in Nehemiah's day was the ministry of Ezra, the teacher of God's law. Not only did the returned exiles benefit from Nehemiah's building ability and Haggai and Zechariah's prophesying, but also from the expounding of the book of the law by Ezra and others who were able to give the meaning so that they understood (Neh. 8:8).

Buried dynamite

Church history tells a similar story. Whenever the Bible has been readily available, understood, and obeyed, the church has prospered. When it has been lost or obscured by tradition, the church has languished. In the Middle Ages the Bible was thought to be too holy for the rank and file to read. Available in a language that only the clergy could understand, it was buried dynamite. When it was eventually translated into the language of the common people and circulated through the invention of the printing press, the spreading of God's Word again became possible. Its explosion shook the religious and political world of that time.

The early disciples were severely criticized for filling Jerusalem with their doctrine. New converts devoted themselves to the apostles' teaching (Acts 2:42). Even after being flogged and threatened, " . . . every day, in the temple and from house to house, they kept right on teaching and preaching Jesus as the Christ" (Acts 5:42).

Jesus Himself had set the example. Even after His resurrection He not only presented Himself alive, but made the disciples' hearts burn within them as He explained in all the Scriptures the things concerning Himself (Luke 24:27). He wanted their faith to rest not simply in the excitement of His post-resurrection appearances but on the sure and certain Word of God.

The importance of the Word to the early church is clear from the Acts record. Luke records that "the word of God increased" (Acts 6:7, RSV); "the word of God grew and multiplied" (Acts 12:24, RSV); "the word of the Lord spread" (Acts 13:49, RSV); "the word of the Lord grew and prevailed mightily" (Acts 19:20, RSV). He describes the growth of the church in terms of the multiplication of the Word.

In the present move of the Holy Spirit, informality and congregational participation ("body ministry") have become valuable features in the meetings. Concern to be "led by the Spirit" has caused some to fear that a prepared message would be liable to quench the Spirit. As we have seen, however, the Scriptures speak of elders laboring in the word (1 Tim. 5:17, RSV). Timothy is encouraged to study, to handle the word of truth aright, and to give himself wholly to the task (2 Tim. 2:15). In the church, Paul tells us, people are not only to bring a tongue, an interpretation, a revelation, a psalm, but also a teaching (1 Cor. 14:26).

"Blessed thoughts"

Without any labor in the Scriptures, spontaneous contributions tend to be superficial or to revolve around a few pet subjects. Alternatively, it becomes simply exhortation of the vaguest kind: "Let's be real! Let's really go on with God!"

What is required of us in sharing the Word? Not that we must always bring a word of "prophetic" significance. In seeking a word "fresh from heaven," simple exposition of the Scriptures can be depreciated as "old hat." Jesus, however, said that every scribe who has become a disciple of the kingdom is like the head of a household, who brings out of his treasure things new and old (Matt. 13:52).

The steward of Jesus' day was a superior slave responsible for the oversight of a family. He maintained stocks sufficient to feed the household with a balanced diet according to their needs. A good teacher will work in a similar fashion, bringing new prophetic words as well as old foundational doctrines in order to build strong lives.

As the preacher reaches for his Bible, he could profitably remember those who lay their hand on that Book and promise "to tell the truth, the whole truth, and nothing but the truth." We do not bless God's people by wrenching verses out of context to prove our point, or by looking for a Bible text to reinforce our preconceived ideas.

Tell it like it is

Nor must we always look for hidden meanings. After hearing some preachers, one almost feels the need of a code book to go with the Bible. With confident assertions that this number or color always represents this or that, they take us on a magical mystery tour of the Bible, leaving the ordinary reader with the feeling that he is quite inadequate ever to plumb its depths. The preacher must make sure he shares what he has received from the Word, not what he has put into it, sharing God's truth, not his own imagination.

If people are to be built up in their holy faith, however, they need more than sermons that only give them information or merely excite their emotions for a while. For a church to function fruitfully the relationship between the pastor and people is very crucial. Ezekiel was told by God that the people listened to him as to one who plays an instrument well or who sings love songs well (Ezek. 33:32). In other words, their appreciation of Ezekiel's ministry was totally unfruitful. They may have been impressed by his ability to communicate, but that was where their response ended.

Congregations often increase in size simply because the preacher is a good communicator. They admire his style, his use of illustrations, his exegesis of the passage, his ability to bring light to obscure texts. Others are warmed by the preaching of an exciting orator who moves the emotions, who draws forth the occasional tear and tugs at the heart strings, sending them away with a warm glow—like one who sings a love song well.

Some relate to their pastors only in this way, and churches are judged by whether they "have a good man" or not. "Does he perform well in the pulpit?" is their chief concern. Others, who may be rather less than Billy Graham in the pulpit, are sometimes redeemed by the fact that they are regarded as having a "nice pastoral ministry" which might be equated with a doctor having a nice bedside manner.

Neither of these gifts (of preaching or caring) is to be despised; they can be a great blessing in the church. There is no virtue in poor communication through shoddy sermon preparation, or a lack of genuine lovingkindness where it is needed. What has to be demolished is the attitude that judges and evaluates pastoral ministry only in these terms. A pastor is a leader. He is responsible for the spiritual life of his sheep. He must not simply be able to impress them from the pulpit, but he must have enough access into the lives of his people to speak directly to them about areas where they fall short, and to encourage and help them in practical matters.

"Heavy shepherding"

Stories abound about the dangers of "heavy shepherding" and authoritarianism among those involved in restoration, but closer inspection reveals churches happy and secure where leaders are honestly and humbly trying to fulfill the New Testament injunction to make disciples and to build up one another in the faith. In reality people do not have to ask permission before making every decision. The leader's goal is like Paul's, to present every man mature—not every man dependent!

As John Stott says:

> There are in *every church* some weak and feeble souls who love to fuss round the minister and are constantly seeking interviews with him to consult him about their spiritual problems.[1] [My italics.]

I wholeheartedly concur with his response to this situation:

> This should be resisted and that strenuously. Gently, but firmly, we should make it clear that God's purpose is that His children should look to Him as their Father and not to men. . . .We long to see the members of our congregation grow up into independent, adult spiritual maturity in Christ, looking to Him for the supply of all their needs since it is "in Christ" that God "has blessed us. . .with every spiritual blessing" (Eph. 1:3).[2]

There simply isn't time to check everybody's wallpaper or holiday arrangements or furniture purchases! Although it seems widespread, the picture of a trembling congregation too frightened to make any decision, somehow mysteriously trapped into a hidebound system from which they cannot escape, does not bear up under investigation.

Within our own congregation in Brighton we have three attorneys, a policeman, several school teachers and businessmen, along with over 500 other adult members who are delighted to be part of an open-style church, but who also rejoice in the fact that the elders lead and the people obey Paul's injunction to know those who are over them in the Lord (1 Thess. 5:12).

They are grateful to God to be able to check out major decisions with their leaders. They see it as God's gracious provision to safeguard them from unnecessary mistakes. They do not feel repressed but released by it. We have all read of the evil events of Jonestown, Guyana, but it is amazing that our simple and honest attempt to respond to the biblical injunction to "obey your leaders" has led some of our evangelical brothers to warn us of the dangers of repeating that horrendous mass suicide. More than one magazine seeking to report what is happening in our ranks has brought this comparison, and it is rather like fearing that England is a police state because one elderly lady was seen being helped over a busy street by an officer of the law. How quick we are to hit the panic button. How quick to fear the worst!

When the local newspaper reported on our own church, they described the people not as nervously submissive and dependent but as follows:

> Gone was the quiet dignity, the soft organ music, the tiptoeing to seats and whispered acknowledgement of neighbors before the service. Everyone seemed to be talking or shouting greetings to friends and about a hundred children were milling around excitedly. . . . As they spilled out into the street after the service, they looked as if they had found a new dimension in their lives. Sunday morning had been a joyous celebration of their faith.[3]

Voluntary submission

The submission to spiritual authority being expressed in churches seeking restoration is totally voluntary. Those handing out hymn books at the door neither carry guns nor possess hypnotic powers. People are simply happy to join churches where there is a sense of involvement that includes genuine discipleship with plenty of checks and balances to safeguard them from error and excess.

In fact, churches that are involved in restoration are committed to building with a team of elders rather than having one pastor. The New Testament always refers to local church elders in the plural, though I am strongly convinced that one of them would be gifted to lead the team as a presiding elder. He will not rule them with an iron fist, but his leadership will release them to operate well together. The alternative is a democratic committee lacking freedom to move with decisiveness.

Elders are not merely Bible college graduates, though they may have gained some helpful theological training, but are men who are gifted and have a calling from God which shows their ability to care for the flock. They must be masters of their own spirit: not self-willed or quick tempered, but gentle and uncontentious, proving their ability to take care of the church of God by the way they manage their own households (1 Tim. 3:2-5). Gone is the formality of the clergy/laity relationship and in its place a true fathering emerges. Special titles are abandoned, giving way to first names. Informality blends with genuine spiritual authority.

"Huge rocks"

Isaiah 32 tells us that leaders will be like huge rocks providing shade in a parched land. They will display stability in the midst of shifting sands. While others seem so changeable, these huge rocks will provide security. You can encounter a rock! A leader will not always agree with you. Sometimes he will hold his ground and you will have to change. A leader's job isn't always to compromise with everybody and keep them happy.

A rock is not easily shaken nor even gradually eroded by persistent pressure. He takes the knocks. He is not quickly moved by every latest fad or paperback (not even this one!).

True leaders do not have to rush around proving that they are leaders and that they have authority. A man who has to argue for his authority clearly does not have any. A huge rock does not need a sign above it saying, *I am a huge rock*. It tends to be self-evident. The real question is, "How big is its shadow?" Do people naturally draw near because of the security it provides?

A true leader does not need to try to get people under his sway, but rests in the confidence that all whom the Father has given him will come to him.

"We are yours"

David, having been secretly anointed by Samuel for leadership, was content to wait for God's time for him to emerge into that leadership role. People gradually came to him in the wilderness. First, the needy came to him for comfort; then, during King Saul's disastrous reign, God began to raise up an army under him. When men joined David they expressed wholehearted commitment to him, so that in turn they were trained and entrusted with positions of authority in his army. As they came to him they said, "We are yours, O David," and promised him loyalty and allegiance.

These men expressed their commitment not only to God's purpose but also to His servant, and it is recorded that this expression of commitment was inspired by the Holy Spirit. It was when the Spirit came upon them that they sang their song of devotion; it was not simply a rush of carnal enthusiasm (1 Chron. 12:18).

Some have argued that they will give themselves only to God, not to leaders of a local church. They have failed to see how God's army will be formed. He will bring bone to bone and join ligaments and sinews together. People joined David's army because the Spirit prompted them to do so. They realized they were living in days when their enemies needed to be overcome and totally subdued. Saul had failed them in this, and now an army was emerging that looked very different.

When people are added to a local church they must sense they are enlisting as soldiers of Christ. All too often, those who desire to serve Christ with this kind of commitment turn their backs on the static and sleepy atmosphere of the local church to join para-church organizations that provide a challenge for them and train them to be soldiers. It is understood that if one applies to such organizations there is a procedure of joining and a commitment required, whereas the local church provides no challenge to be considered when joining.

If local churches are going to become communities of friends who want to express loyalty to Christ and to one another and to be trained for the warfare to which Jesus called us, it is vital that they know who belongs to that community and on what basis they are joining.

"My feet are within Your gates"

Because there is great variety of understanding in what is meant by Christian commitment and church membership, many churches have introduced what might be called an introductory class or commitment series. This is not to be confused with a class for discipling. Its goal is not to produce a certain degree of maturity which qualifies the applicant for entry. It is more a time for explanation of what is meant by true repentance, faith, and other aspects of individual conversion. Also, it explains to the new-comer what is meant by commitment to a particular body of believers.

A program of some eight weeks provides an opportunity for Bible study and open discussion, at the end of which people are free to ask for church membership if they so desire, and, of course, are free to withdraw and become members elsewhere if they do not seek such involvement.

By this approach we show that it is no insignificant thing to be added to a local church. Nehemiah was appalled and brokenhearted when he heard that the walls of Jerusalem were broken down and its gates burned. Anyone could stroll in and out of Zion. A major work of restoration was involved in rebuilding the walls and repairing the gates.

The elders then had the responsibility of guarding the gates.

Jesus described himself as both the Good Shepherd and the Door. Those entering the church must come through Him. In a local church the elders or pastors should provide the way into their flock; and people should join, not by climbing up over the wall, but through a genuine relationship with the elders, acknowledging their right to keep the door of the church.

Count me in!

When an individual joins a local church he should not only see himself as joining a company of believers but also as placing himself within the sphere of a particular group of elders or pastors. By joining their flock he becomes one for whom they feel a sense of responsibility. They have to care for him. Their aim should be to build him up in the faith and present him mature to Christ. They will have to give account to God for him. This calls for a clear relationship to be formed between pastors and people.

These principles have largely been forgotten in the church of God. An explanation at the outset through a "commitment course" provides opportunity for potential new members to understand what the New Testament order is. It is explained to them that the church is a body of disciples forming a community of love; it is not simply a meeting place providing services at certain set times.

A commitment course provides an opportunity to explain to prospective new members that, if they join that particular congregation, they will be joining as disciples of Christ and not simply as "churchgoers." They will, therefore, want their lives to be discipled and will welcome not only encouragement and objective teaching but also, where necessary, admonition and specific words of correction. Believing that "faithful are the wounds of a friend" (Prov. 27:6), they commit themselves to that kind of relationship.

As in marriage, the relationship is two-way. The elders express their desire to love and serve the people and fulfill their role as leaders, and the people declare their desire to follow, to be discipled and built into the body where their gifts may be used to the glory of God.

What about the church meeting?

From some with denominational backgrounds we might hear the question, "Don't you have church business meetings where you vote about things?" The answer would have to be, "Yes and no."

At my home church we have what we call "Family Evenings," not to vote about issues but to share with the family the vision for the future and any particular decisions that currently are being made. Such meetings do not happen regularly (say quarterly, as with some churches) but whenever there is a need. Some months may elapse without one, and then we may find the need for several such meetings in a comparatively short time (though many issues are regularly shared at church prayer meetings).

The Family Evening is not a decision-making occasion but provides opportunity for views to be expressed. Normally elders will reach a decision together and then share that with the home-group leaders before bringing it to the church. By that time a significant number of responsible people in the church have had opportunity to discuss the issues involved.

Different matters require different treatment. Having planned renovations on our church building, we invited observations from the church family. Original ideas drawn up by elders were significantly changed as a result of recommendations made by church members. With regard to spiritual issues, however, elders would see it as their responsibility to lead. Wise shepherds will always be listening to their flock anyway, and elders' decisions may well have their origin in the insights of other church members.

When I was first converted and then became a member of a local church, I was profoundly shocked at the atmosphere of the church business meeting. It was so different from the Sunday services! People were outspokenly angry, and the godly pastor's single vote had no more authority than anyone else's. This amazed me, since it was evident that his God-given anointing had gathered and blessed the large congregation. He was obviously qualified to lead the flock. Instead of appreciating their pastor's thoroughbred stock, though, these people apparently considered him to have a dubious track record. On the whole, church business meetings were not happy places to be.

Family evenings

We enjoy our Family Evenings. A great time of praise and prophesying usually opens the way. We applaud new members, and other domestic news is often greeted with cheers and laughter. Then the main item of that particular evening is handled. It may be the annual accounts, or plans for further extension work, house-group reshuffles, intended new eldership appointments, and so on. Many or few matters may be covered, and there may be the sort of item that Jesus said was so serious that we must "tell it to the church" (Matt. 18:17). We do not despise the "church meeting" but rejoice in it and its new style. The flock feels secure with its shepherds and believes it is going somewhere as it follows its leaders.

CHAPTER 9

Church-based Evangelism

*T*here was a time when churches seeking restoration were very vulnerable to the criticism that they were inward-looking. It was argued that they had become little charismatic clubs demonstrating no evangelistic concern but simply rejoicing in their spiritual gifts. A superficial glance in our direction convinced many that this was the case, and in some ways they were justified in their conclusion. Let me explain how I, for one, turned my back on the lost for a while.

I was raised in a strongly evangelistic setting, and when I left my secular job it was to do the work of evangelism. As I have said, I preached on Brighton seafront, went from door to door, and was very involved in coffee bar evangelism. While at London Bible College I was elected Evangelistic Chairman for the student body.

It was no surprise, then, that when I took up my first pastorate I introduced a very full program of evangelism. We held a gospel service every Sunday night. We visited from door to door. We rented our own downtown coffee bar. We visited the pubs, witnessing and singing. We ran evangelistic barbecues. We showed a series of Billy Graham films and also invited evangelists to conduct crusades in the town. This is by no means an exhaustive list of the many different approaches used, and all of them were backed with a strong emphasis on prayer and intercession. The lasting results of our endeavors, however, could not even be termed negligible. They were virtually nonexistent. People were contacted and sometimes even came to church for a while, but only fell away again after a short time.

Net mending

One night at a prayer meeting God spoke to us in prophecy and said we should "mend the nets." We interpreted this to mean that there were holes in the framework of our relationships as a church that made us ineffective in catching men for Christ. We therefore gave ourselves to resolving our many internal problems. We stopped all our special evangelistic efforts and even canceled our Sunday evening gospel service. Gradually, we began to enjoy the fruits of developing loving relationships within our ranks. Also, our meetings gradually became quite exciting, with worship moving into new dimensions of joy and freedom. Some began to join us, being attracted by what we were discovering, and gradually we began to grow.

At that time an attractive doctrine was promulgated suggesting that if we "got the church right" the people would be pressing at our doors to get in. I confess that I, for one, accepted this new "revelation" for a while, though my strong evangelistic background provoked some inner conflicts. But the fact was that we were now growing without reaching out. We even tended to yield to the temptation of regarding evangelism as "old hat" and would refer to "all that striving in the old days."

Closer inspection, however, would have revealed that our growth was not through new birth but almost entirely through Christians changing address! What I began to see was that if we "got the church right" people really would be pressing at our doors to get in; but, in the main, the importunate were thirsty Christians. The vast numbers of the unconverted did not come near our door to inquire. They knew nothing of the changes taking place within.

Poaching

There have been those who have criticized our growth, calling it "poaching." But a poacher deliberately breaks into another person's territory, stealing their property. This has not been our style, nor has it been necessary. There is a widespread move of the Holy Spirit in the church today, and hungry and thirsty Christians are looking for places which are not only built firmly on God's Word, but are also open to the life of the Holy Spirit.

But this is not the end of the story. For nowadays evangelism is, once again, one of our major preoccupations. Obviously, there is the danger of generalizing, but my experience is quite wide, and this is what I have observed: An over-preoccupation with "net-mending" can result in our forgetting what nets are for. We could move on from mending them to embroidering them and hanging them on the walls for decoration. But nets are for catching fish.

There has been an honest acknowledgement of the fact that most of our growth had presented no numerical threat to Satan's kingdom, since most of our new members had already been saved before they joined us. This led to a growing prayer burden, and I have observed two resulting developments.

Natural growth

Evangelism is partly the natural outworking of the life of a healthy local church. As many within our ranks have had encounters with God, their whole spiritual life has been enlarged, and a desire to win others has gradually emerged. Also, many who have been Christians for several years have had their lives so changed that unconverted relatives have witnessed the breakthrough, and have started to come to see what this is all about. This has led to many conversions.

Christians of years' standing who later on have been filled with the Holy Spirit have immediately asked to be baptized. Unconverted relatives have come to witness the baptism, and some have gone home from the baptismal service converted. So a chain reaction begins.

Gifted evangelists

This is not the whole story, however, for Jesus ascended on high and gave gifts to his church: some apostles, some prophets, some evangelists, and some pastors and teachers (Eph. 4:7-13). For the church to come to full measure we must see all these gifts fully functioning, and our need of the evangelist is very real. If evangelism was only "the natural growth of the body" we would not need the gift of the evangelist, but Jesus has supplied him, so we obviously need him.

Others may have been led differently, but in Brighton we simply acknowledged our need and asked Mike Sprenger, a local Campus Crusade evangelist, to come among us and spend some time training us in personal evangelism and in getting us out onto the streets. I then met Ben Davies, a Baptist minister from Bracknell, who spoke at our local ministers' group on the theme of church-based evangelism. His zeal stirred something deep in my spirit, and I asked him to come and speak to us. The results of his visits to the churches I serve has been considerable. Though at the moment his title designates him a pastor, his anointing and motivation is largely as an evangelist.

What is the evangelist's role? I believe it is two-fold. Obviously he is himself an able communicator of the gospel and one who wins souls; but, according to Ephesians 4:12, he also equips the saints for the work of ministry. In other words, he does not simply arrive on the scene to do it all for us, but rather comes to motivate and mobilize local churches into the work of evangelism.

He will come as a provocation. He will warn us of our complacency. We may be large and flourishing, we may be enjoying wonderful, flowing worship and fellowship at a level we had never known before, but what about the lost? What about the commandment to go and be witnesses? Not only will he challenge us; he will teach us how to do it. He will equip us with motivation and methods. An evangelist moving freely among churches open to his ministry will be a constant source of inspiration. He should not be a stranger who simply comes to town to put on his show in the area and looks to the local churches to back him up.

I do not say this in order to attack evangelists. God knows how much we need them! Rather, my challenge is to churches to make room for them to fulfill a ministry that can have more lasting fruit in and through the churches. Build relationships with evangelists! Open your doors to them. Let them in to disturb and equip you! Just as the pastor has needed to see his role changed, so must the evangelist. He is no longer simply to fill the pulpit, but is also to produce after his kind through discipling within the churches.

Evangelistic churches

Although it is evident that the mighty evangelist, Billy Graham, is bearing lasting fruit throughout the world by mass evangelism, Howard Snyder's comment at the Lausanne Congress must still be heard. "The church is the *only* divinely-appointed means of spreading the Gospel . . . .Evangelism makes little sense divorced from the fact of the Christian community."[1] The church is both the agent and the goal of evangelism. The evangelistic crusade that is not church-centered usually proves to be a bag with holes. Later inspection can often show very little remaining of those who responded to the preaching. Evangelists may have had thousands through their counseling rooms throughout a year's ministry, but the acid test still remains—how many were added to local churches? The Bible talks about people being "added" rather than simply converted, and it is debatable whether we should regard people as truly added before they become functioning members of a local body.

"Come and join us"

True conversion cannot be seen as separate from being added to the people of God, and this not simply in a hidden, mystical way, but in an evident and practical way. The invitation is to flee one society and be added to another (Acts 2:40-41), and the outward demonstration of response according to the Scriptures is baptism in water. There has been considerable debate on the value of an invitation system and whether or not we call men to stand, raise their hand, come to the front, or pray the penitent prayer. The Bible has a straightforward answer. Be baptized! Interdenominational crusades encounter major problems when baptism is mentioned, but the New Testament is clear that this is God's prescribed response for the sinner. Church-based evangelism has no problem in this area.

We do not simply want to send inquirers away with some Christian literature; we want to see them come under Jesus' lordship. We also want them to have a dynamic experience of God Himself. In our gospel presentation, therefore, we are "up front" with the matter of baptism and receiving the Holy Spirit. We feel no freedom to offer an emaciated gospel devoid of the content so obviously present in the New Testament. New Testament evangelists did not invite people to consider if they would like to obey the Lord in the matter of baptism. They baptized them! When Cornelius and his companions were filled with the Holy Spirit, Peter ordered them to be baptized (Acts 10:48). Paul received similar treatment from Ananias (Acts 22:16). Those arguing that they are not quite sure whether they want to be baptized are clearly saying they are not quite sure whether to acknowledge Jesus as their Lord. Surely this is a totally inadequate response to our glorious King.

Quality of life

Our standards of evangelism are deeply affected by the quality of life within a local church. If the church has a clear commitment to becoming disciples of Jesus Christ and has a developed community life, the gospel call, by implication, has far more content, and responding to Christ has far greater significance. People being saved in our setting realize that they are joining a community, a people, a nation, not just finding a personal Savior. We do not have all things in common (Acts 2:44) or live in special community houses, nor do we feel that God is leading us in that direction; but we are trying to build our lives together as intimately as possible while safeguarding the family unit. When someone is added, they are not added to the back of the line— they help make up the circle.

The prominent place that free and expressive worship holds in our services clearly has evangelistic impact. Many have been converted in the context of charismatic praise. They have had an immediate encounter with God and have sometimes had their hearts revealed by a word of knowledge from a member of the church before any preaching took place. Several churches have reintroduced special gospel meetings. They immediately face the question, "Shall we change our style of worship for the sake of the outsider?" The conclusion has been rather to offer some explanation at the outset of the service, but essentially to let the praise flow freely. We are finding that many are being saved in our morning worship, as well as in our evening gospel/baptismal services.

Churches have even taken to the streets, not only with gospel proclamation, but also with praise and dance. As that great evangelist, David Watson, said, "A praising community preaches to answer questions raised by its praise"[2]— a good summary of Acts 2.

Friends of sinners

One of the church's greatest problems in evangelism is that we have so lost touch with the world—in terms of natural contact— that a strong "come out of the world" call, reinforced by a legalistic approach to the "no-go areas," has left many Christians in total isolation from the world. Rediscovery of our deliverance from both Old Testament law as a way of salvation, and evangelical law as a way of being acceptable, releases us to break into the sinner's territory as Jesus did.

A brother I am closely associated with, who leads a flourishing church in Kent, recently rented a local wine bar and invited contacts to a meal (yes, with wine!) where the gospel was clearly shared. Most of the people had first been befriended at the local golf club, which the pastor and his church members have infiltrated with considerable gospel impact. There are many evening classes, keep-fit clubs, and various sports organizations that can be joined, not only for the fulfillment of being there, but also for the gospel's sake. We must break out of our evangelical ghettos.

The house groups have proved to be another very fruitful sphere for evangelism. Though normally used for the expression of our covenant life in God, they can easily be temporarily transformed into evangelistic settings for special outreach efforts. Contacts are invited to open evenings where it is made clear in advance that at the end of the supper (or whatever is planned) two or three will tell why they have personal faith in God today.

Gradually the whole atmosphere of church life becomes evangelistic. Numbers are being added to churches to such a degree that buildings are becoming full. Where do we go from here? Happily, we started not with the goal of filling the building but filling the earth, so the fact of our overcrowding is greeted with rejoicing, not dismay.

Start again

The way forward is to send out another congregation and start all over again. Several of the churches with which I am involved have started new congregations either on the other side of town, from where their people were already coming, or, indeed, in the next town.

We found that our own congregation was drawn from all over the Brighton and Hove urban area. When we had become about 500 committed adults plus nearly 200 teenagers and children, we asked about 200 who were traveling from Brighton every Sunday to form a new congregation in their area. A school hall was found, and we started again.

We began in a small school hall in Hove. Our ultimate goal was not simply to fill a large church building, which we later acquired and renovated, but to fill the Brighton and Hove area. So we hope to see congregations burgeon all over the area until thousands are brought in, and we can actually begin to drop the word "added" and start using that other exciting New Testament word, "multiplied."

Initially, the new church is cared for by the same group of elders leading the original work. As time goes by, however, the second work becomes self-sufficient, though obviously retaining the intimate links of fellowship already built, and being cared for by the same apostolic ministry.

But more of this in a later chapter, where we will consider the role of the apostle today. First, we shall consider the prophet.

CHAPTER 10

Prophetic Vision

*B*ill had been pastoring Old Town Baptist Church for three difficult years. Though there were encouragements, with several opening their hearts to charismatic life, internal problems continually sapped his energies, and, like hidden icebergs, threatened to sink the ship. Where was he taking the ship anyway? He wasn't too sure.

He set aside for himself three days of prayer and fasting, at the end of which he felt he had a clear sense of direction. He could not wait to bring his new revelation to the church and excitedly shared his new plans with the deacons.

"We've never done that kind of thing here," said the senior deacon.

"People are not willing to see those kinds of changes," said another.

"Perhaps we could try it next year," the church secretary offered.

"If you do that, I know the Robinsons will leave, and we can't afford that," said the church treasurer, who went on to remind Bill that he was a comparative newcomer and that many people had been members years before he arrived.

Bill's spirits gradually sank. Two weeks later, after a further time of prayer, he preached an anger-filled sermon giving off more heat than light. The deacons, offended, took him aside and warned him that he must settle down or move on.

Bill always found the Area Superintendent a sympathetic man.

He soon found Bill another church, and after a few months the announcement was made that Bill felt led by God to become pastor of the church at New Town.

Exposure to the prophets

This could so easily have been my own experience, but in 1972, when we had come as far as we could, God graciously brought across my path two mighty prophetic ministers who influenced my life greatly.

I attended a conference called by Arthur Wallis on the subject of the ministries listed in Ephesians 4:11, particularly that of the prophet. A brother I did not know stood to speak, and his word gripped me from beginning to end. Though he was asked to speak on the prophet's role, he did more than that. He fulfilled the prophet's ministry by thrilling my heart with the vision of a triumphant and glorious church, "a city set on a hill, which cannot be hid." I cannot now remember all that he said; but I well remember how my heart burned within me, and the essential vision has never left me.

As soon as the conference ended I approached him and asked, "Would you please come and speak for a week at my church?" He responded warmly, and the date was fixed: he would speak at our church's fourth anniversary.

In preparation for his visit the church had a day of prayer and fasting. During this we were encouraged by a vision one of the women had. She saw a dirty, cracked old cup, out of whose center rose a beautiful, new, shining chalice. This, I believe, is prophetic of the church worldwide, but it also helped us to understand what was happening to us, and why.

Breakthrough

David's visit proved to be a time of breakthrough. As the week progressed he enlarged our expectation for the immediate presence of God, and he brought us from a legalistic kind of zeal into the freedom of the sons of God, who know their Father loves them. God also crowned his ministry among us with some remarkable healings.

There was no reluctance to "go to church" that week! In fact, no one wanted to stay away and risk missing something else that God might say or do. Any remaining inhibitions about raising our hands and shouting praise were irrelevant; exuberant worship was a natural response to the truth bursting upon us. "The truth shall make you free"; and the truths that God loves us unconditionally and forever, that He chose us because He wants us, that He wants us to be in constant companionship with Him—these liberated us from chains of legalism and cold formality.

I will always associate one particular song with that glorious week. It was based on Psalm 126, and it perfectly described our feelings:

When the Lord turned again the captivity of Zion
We were like those who dream
Then was our mouth filled with laughter,
And our tongue with singing.

At the end of the week the leaders enjoyed a meal together prior to the final meeting. One of the men went ahead to unlock the church building. As he left, we joked that he had a "church-unlocking ministry." On reflection I realized that this was an apt description of David's ministry to us. He had released us from a puny, parochial vision and had enlarged our horizon as only a prophet could. He had lifted us individually and corporately into a new dimension.

A prophetic people

We had begun to grasp God's intentions for the church; we began to become a prophetic people. Many a congregation contains good people, but they are not sufficiently exposed to the prophetic ministry, and so fail to be excited by God's ultimate purpose. Short-term problems dominate their thinking and prevent radical change. Even in the midst of spiritual renewal, such congregations fail to grasp what the renewing is for and where God is taking them.

We need the prophet's voice to come like an axe to the root of our problems. Many churches are beset by layers of tangled undergrowth that prevent light and growth and also cover deeply rooted fears, misconceptions, and ignorance. The prophet has the incisive clarity of vision to cut through clutter, to search out motives and intentions like a probing laser beam. He forces us to ask uncomfortable questions that lead to uncomfortable answers. He causes the leaders to reexamine the church's activities in the light of the principles he shows them. Often the diagnosis demands drastic surgery that the elders would have shrunk from on their own, even if they had fully perceived the nature of the problem.

Sometimes the prophet's message appears to be hard and unkind when it insists, "No compromise." But this message comes from a heart burning with zeal for God's church and with desire for her to be a pure bride.

Not an expositor

A prophet is not simply a preacher, though he will preach. He is not simply an expositor of the Bible, though his great burden will be to bring us back to the Word and its authority. He is a seer, a man of vision. Abraham's prophetic gaze stretched down through the centuries; he was transfixed by the "city which has foundations" (Heb. 11:10). Moses was similarly impelled by his vision, and he brought out from bondage a people whose very existence was rooted in his prophetic gift (Hos. 12:13). The Hebrews in turn became a light to the nations—a prophetic people.

The prophet must have room to move, not just by speaking at large conferences, but by coming into our churches. We must be prepared for him to expose our weakness and need so that it can be changed. We need not fear that his ministry is only concerned with tearing down. It is also for building up and equipping the saints and for instilling in them a glorious panoramic vision of God's intentions for the church. People will be much more willing to lay aside every weight, hindrance, and unnecessary baggage if they are excited by the goal toward which they are running. A church that is exposed to prophetic ministry will become uncompromising in its commitment to obey God's revealed will, whatever the implications of that obedience may be.

When Ezra and his colleagues returned to Zion to rebuild the temple, their initial zeal began to flag in the face of opposition and difficulty; but we are told that when Haggai and Zechariah began to prophesy, the people's sights were lifted, and they began to work with new understanding and faith.

Prophetic inspiration

A rebuilding program can be a hard, unrelenting slog against a backdrop of considerable hostility and misrepresentation. Nehemiah and the faithful others had to contend with the challenge of threats, mockery, lies, compromise, and internal disloyalty. Meanwhile, they were daily building the wall opposite to their homes. When they saw only a little wall, slowly growing, they could easily have been tempted to dismay. But when the prophets came on the scene, describing the glories of God's ultimate purpose and assuring them of His absolute commitment to them, they found fresh resources of energy with which to build. Prophets have the ability to lift our small local endeavors into the larger scene.

Prophets bring to the people revelation and clarity concerning God's purpose for their time. Jeremiah, for instance, had to burst the balloon of false trust in outward religion, calling Judah to true dependence on God, not just on His temple (Jer. 7:4). While they continued depending on their traditions as if they had all the time in the world, Jeremiah had to warn them that their time was rapidly running out.

Haggai similarly challenged those of his generation who failed to comprehend that it was time to rebuild the house of the Lord (Hag. 1:2).

Prophetic vision

"Without vision the people perish"; and they also get sidetracked into preoccupation with present worries and relative trivialities. Every time the children of Israel complained about the monotony of their diet they demonstrated their lack of vision for God's purpose. Without vision people also lose faith. God had said He would bring the Hebrew people into a land flowing with milk and honey, but they often lost sight of this goal; and when that happened, they were so threatened by circumstances that they talked of being brought into the wilderness to die. They lived only in the short term. Many who thank God today for their deliverance from spiritual Egypt have no concept of God's purpose to bring them into Canaan.

Unfortunately, many people today think of Canaan only in terms of going to heaven when they die. In Moses' understanding (Exod. 15:17), what lay beyond the Jordan was the land, the city, and the temple: a land to be possessed, Zion to be populated, and a temple where God's presence could be enjoyed and His praise expressed. Out of Zion would go light to the world!

What do you see?

Clarity of vision keeps us from activity that is not centered in the ultimate goal. God often asked the prophets, "What do you see?" What you see will determine what you build. Zechariah replied that he saw one gold lampstand with a supernatural energy supply (Zech. 4:2). Though his prophecy is found in what we call the Old Testament, he was actually a prophet of the new covenant. He saw one glorious church as the light of the world, working not by might, nor by power, but by God's Spirit.

When the vision of the kingdom of God fills our horizon, it will affect our whole lifestyle, our values, our decisions. As a young Christian I was taught no true vision for the church. Raised on dispensationalism, I was told that we were living in the Laodicean age, and that the Lord's return was our only hope. Meanwhile, if anyone heard Jesus knocking at the door of his heart, there was always the wonder of personal salvation. Glorious news! I was truly thankful for it. But the whole emphasis of our evangelical life was "personal." We had a "personal" Savior, practiced "personal" evangelism, and pursued "personal" devotions.

No one told me that God had promised His Son the nations as His inheritance and the ends of the earth as His possession (Ps. 2:8), or that the increase of His government would know no end (Isa. 9:7), and that the saints of the Most High would receive the kingdom and possess it forever (Dan. 7:18), and that these glorious promises somehow included me!

Though our church was keen on missionary work, it was never taught, "He will bring forth justice to the nations . . . .He will not be disheartened or crushed, until He has established justice in the earth; and the coastlands will wait expectantly for His law" (Isa. 42:1,4). Missionary work consisted of isolated stabs at Satan's strongholds.

Now, however, we are beginning to understand the great implications of these magnificent prophetic statements for the church and for the nations of the world. Although gross darkness covers the earth, we realize that "Arise, shine, for your light has come" is not a poetic challenge for a far-off time, but is a call to us now! A sense of destiny, glorious and triumphant, fills our hearts with a driving force. This revelation is reflected in many of our songs, which are no longer about a poor, beleaguered, battered church that waits helplessly to be rescued, but now tell of God's army, filled with His power, bright with banners and marching to victory.

Beware "triumphalism"

At the same time we have to beware of the dangers of a superficial "triumphalism" that says we glide through life unhindered by tragedy, disappointment, difficulties, or dangers. From now on, all is plain sailing, and to admit to problems is tantamount to failure and backsliding. There is no justification at all in Scripture for this sort of thinking. We are told quite clearly that "through many tribulations we must enter the kingdom of God" (Acts

14:22). But it is our perspective on life that has been revolution-
ized, helping us to persevere through the pressures.

People's lives have to change when they encounter and
embrace the prophetic vision. The prophet has the ability to take
the ancient prophecies and make them relevant to the twentieth
century. Within our ranks many have turned down promotions
for the sake of the kingdom, and have been willing to jeopardize
their careers if to advance them meant being transferred to a place
where there was no clear gospel witness to join, where they could
work out the principles God has planted in their hearts. Others
have been stirred by God to move in order to help pioneer new
works. All our values have to be reassessed. Are we going for the
one pearl beyond price, or are we taken up with lesser gems?

Second, prophets; third, teachers

Some have tried to dismiss the prophetic gift by arguing that a
prophet is simply a preacher or teacher, but the lists of gifts in
Ephesians 4:11, 1 Corinthians 12:28, and Romans 12:6-7 are
consistent in differentiating between them. Why does the Holy
Spirit record them as different if they are simply the same gift? And
what are we missing in the church without their ministry?

I thank God for the impact of the Bible Weeks in England,
where the vision of God's prophetic purposes has been expressed. The Capel Bible Week in the seventies set a pattern,
drawing hundreds from churches around the country. But since
then we have seen thousands pouring into other areas of Britain,
to other Bible Weeks where the prophetic word can be heard.
Because churches are encouraged to camp together there is the
potential for whole congregations to be transformed by the
Weeks' ministry.

Open the church

The fact remains, however, that the local church must itself be
exposed to the prophet's ministry. Apostles and prophets are of
foundational importance there. Personally, I am not looking for

prophets in the Old Testament mold who will knock on the door of the Prime Minister's house to proclaim what the nation's attitude should be toward the NATO alliance. I am looking, rather, for prophets who will so affect local church life that the church itself becomes a prophetic voice to the nation, calling it to repent and believe the gospel. The New Testament prophet speaks essentially to the church, not to the heathen nation in which the church dwells—though his message has far-reaching social and political impact.

Without the prophet the local church will lack the vision, motivation, and faith to fulfill its God-given role. When an exclusively pastoral foundation is laid in a local church, that company will fail to be truly charismatic, even if many become Spirit-filled, speak in tongues, and sing the song of the Lord.

The prophet must not be invited simply to excite the people occasionally, but to equip the saints and to produce the fruit of his own ministry in their lives. He will see where death has crept into a situation and where discouragement has resulted in the congregation simply going through the motions of religious life without any expectation.

"Take courage, Joshua!"

During the restoration program in the Old Testament, the prophets spoke not only to the people but to leaders such as Joshua and Zerubbabel, who were awakened to a new sense of their calling and appointment by Haggai and Zechariah. So today prophets will not simply bring sermons to the congregation, but will develop relationships whereby leaders derive great encouragement from their ministry.

In my first church we were pressing on with new zeal and joy as a result of David's visit (the prophet spoken of earlier), but we were still not free from internal problems. Now another prophet came among us. He had been speaking nearby at a Saturday night celebration, and I warmly responded to the suggestion that he preach on Sunday morning. We did not know one another, though I had heard him preach once before, and liked what I heard.

During our time of open worship, Alex stood and prophesied. At first his words were warm and encouraging; then they became very specific. "You, My sons, who oppose the work of My Spirit in this place: Unless you change your heart, you will be removed from this place, and your ministry will be removed from you. Young men, prepare yourselves for ministry. For in this place My hand shall increasingly be upon My shepherd, and I shall increasingly call him out to minister here and there in My service. In this place he shall grow less and less, and you shall grow more and more. Young men, prepare yourselves for ministry."

We all trembled. Alex had described in detail what had been happening in our midst. His prophecies concerning the future also proved amazingly accurate. As I walked to lunch with him I asked, "Alex, who told you about us? How did you know what we were going through?" "I didn't," he replied, "but during the worship God showed me a vision and gave me the word."

Everything Alex prophesied did indeed happen, and the people understood that God had been among us. It was not human manipulation that was leading us along, but the living God. The impact of the prophetic ministry was amazing.

"Thou art the man!"

Some prophetic ministry paints a large vision of what is going to happen, inspiring us to new acts of faith and delivering us from the commonplace. We come to understand that the church has a glorious destiny. "The mountain of the house of the Lord will be established as the chief of the mountains, and will be raised above the hills; and all the nations will stream to it" (Isa. 2:2). Through the difficulties, we excitedly press on as a prophetic people.

Other prophetic ministry concentrates the mind in different directions. "Thou art the man," it says, and uncovers our hypocrisy, giving us opportunity to repent so that we can face the future with hope.

We must make room for prophets. During the period of the Judges, there came a time when the people were overwhelmed by the hosts of Midian and began to cry out to God. His first answer was to raise a prophetic voice that pinpointed the root of their problem. He then moved on to raise a new anointed leader in Gideon, gathering around him a newly committed army. The same pattern was seen when God raised up through Samuel the anointed leader, David, and his invincible band. Again we see the pattern when God raised up John the Baptist, who preceded God's anointed leader, our Lord Jesus, who drew around Him an army of disciples. God is today raising up a new army committed to anointed leadership, one that is rooted in prophetic vision.

When I was speaking at a ministers' conference in South Africa, I was asked about the details of what makes home groups flourish. The questioner was looking for one magic ingredient to bring success to his existing framework, and he felt that house groups might work well. What he failed to see was that this system is part of a whole prophetic vision. House groups on their own are not enough. Change has to be much more radical if there is to be lasting fruit.

Unbalanced

Listening to a prophet is unlike listening to a teacher. The prophet will sometimes sound unbalanced: for a while he will sound as though he has only one message. His burden will be not to make sure that the balance is correct but that the present issue is being resolved. It will be the local elders' responsibility to work out the detailed implications of the grand sweep of the prophetic vision. The prophet may create problems when he comes, but his visit is worthwhile. As we respond to him we become prophetic people for our own generation.

The prophet, a man of prayer, will direct us back to God. A church influenced by a prophet will become a praying community: not merely going through the routine of prayer, but releasing the power of God through powerful corporate intercession.

CHAPTER 11

A House of Prayer

What a sight it must have been! Tables upturned, coins scattered, livestock fleeing, and Jesus standing with whip in hand at the center of all the commotion.

Dismissing the religious facade of special temple money and sacrifices, He declared the temple "a robber's den." Then, full of zeal for His Father's house, He reminded them of God's word on the matter: "My house shall be called a house of prayer" (Matt. 21:13).

Jesus surely could have described the house of God in many other ways, so we should take serious note of this particular title. Prayer is seen as the distinctive feature of the house of God. Now we are His house (Heb. 3:6), and the question must be faced: to what degree could our corporate life be called a house of prayer?

A few years ago one would often assess the spiritual zeal of a local church by looking at its notice board to see if and when it held prayer meetings. I was raised in a church which had two evening prayer meetings in its weekly program, and I followed that pattern in my first pastorate. Sadly, these prayer meetings were often formal and lifeless. As time went by, God began to speak to us about the essential place of small groups in our body life, and the home-group system replaced church prayer meetings and Bible-study evenings.

Though these home meetings were to include prayer, we made it perfectly clear that they were not prayer meetings. Their purpose was more diverse, covering many aspects of our corporate life. Prayer in these groups has often centered more around the personal needs and aspirations of group members. This has proved a great and necessary blessing in knitting the lives of the members together more intimately. Formality has disappeared as people have opened their hearts to one another.

At this point one might level the criticism that we are no longer essentially a house of prayer. A house of fellowship, yes, or even a house of praise, but not a house of prayer. Now God has impressed on us the need to reintroduce corporate prayer, not in place of our home-group life but in addition to it.

Spiritual warfare

There is a growing sense of spiritual warfare among us; the word "revival" has been on our lips again. If we are going to see the mighty move of God that lifts us to another place in His purposes, we will have to develop in intercession.

"Why prayer is so indispensable we cannot say, but we had better recognize the fact even if we cannot explain it," wrote J.O. Fraser, the mighty pioneer missionary who worked so powerfully for God among the Lisu tribes of China some sixty years ago, resulting in the conversion of thousands.

Fraser had a highly developed understanding of the power of prayer, and he approached the matter very pragmatically when he said:

We often speak of intercessory work as being of vital importance. I want to prove that I believe this in actual fact by giving my first and best energies to it as God may lead. I feel like a businessman who perceives that a certain line of goods pays better than any other in his store and who purposes making it his chief investment.[1]

Praying churches

The church prayer meeting having been temporarily abandoned, its rediscovery had to be in keeping with all that God had taught us in intervening years.

We begin our prayer meetings with praise, seeing the Lord high and lifted up above all our needs and longings, able to supply every answer. But we remember on such occasions that we have come primarily to intercede. Without this discipline we can easily get carried away with praise (a glorious preoccupation!), and thus find no time to ask, seek, and knock. By all means we let our evening be punctuated by moments of believing praise. Then we return to the job in hand with disciplined purpose. When we have the assurance that we have been heard, we conclude the time with a confident shout of thanksgiving.

It goes without saying that we must be a people of true unity of heart to release power in prayer, not seeking to impress with our eloquence nor imposing guilt with our burden, nor despising the faltering words of those new to the experience. Eloquence too often can replace child-like and genuine faith, while the newest convert can often bring a note of unvarnished reality that helps us all break through. The prayer meeting, therefore, must be a place where genuine love is expressed.

Sometimes we do not have enough time to wait for everyone to add their prayers consecutively, so we feel free to raise our voices together in pursuit of our motive. God can untangle our cries. Then someone may find the anointing to lead in prayer in summary of our corporate burden.

Teach and pray

To get a sense of direction for corporate prayer, elders must be open before God; and they must be unafraid to lead, letting others catch their burden. It is often through the lack of clear goals that prayer dissipates. Where relationships are well formed and love prevails, leadership is able to bring teaching and admonition to those who pray "off-center" prayers, or who want to include every burden in one long list of a prayer. Without instruction we fail to see issues through.

We are in a battle. Often we need to hold our ground until faith assures us we have what we ask for. The fact that someone "just prayed my prayer" is no reason for you not to pray it as well. Joash learned from Elisha that sometimes, to prevail in warfare, you must strike five or six times, not giving up after three attempts (2 Kings 13:19).

An awareness of spiritual conflict sometimes calls us to our feet so we can corporately resist the devil and use the authority God has given us to bind and loose spiritual forces. Learning to use the weapons of our warfare, which are able to pull down enemy strongholds, we become increasingly aware of ourselves as an army, moving together in throwing back the powers of darkness and bringing in the rule of Christ through militant faith.

Open to the Holy Spirit

There will be times when we discern that the wind of the Spirit is beginning to blow in another direction as we pray. For example, I recently announced at a church prayer meeting that our main burden must be to pray for more elders to be raised up. Yet, after a time of praise, we quickly found that the Holy Spirit was stirring us strongly to pray for the lost to be saved. This was not simply one person's deep concern being imposed on the group (a factor to be watched), but was a widespread feeling. We therefore abandoned the eldership theme and followed the Holy Spirit.

The gifts of the Holy Spirit are not playthings here but are powerful weapons in the battle. Visions and prophecies often lead us in the conflict and give us a sense of direction.

Elders should be guiding and instructing their people throughout such prayer times. If, for instance, a congregation is praying for $50,000 in next Sunday's special offering, they should be reminded that God has led them on the course that requires this sum, and that He is faithful. They may ask that everyone be faithful in giving, and that each might know specifically what his contribution should be; and then, having considered their apparently inadequate resources, they should cast their burden on the God of the miraculous, who is able to multiply these "loaves and fishes." Having prayed for a while, people can stop and ask one another if they have faith for it: do they have assurance yet?

The church may then ask God together, "Would you please give us $50,000 next Sunday?", exercising child-like corporate faith followed by a shout of praise and worship. When $50,000 is raised the following Sunday, the joy in the congregation knows no bounds. We have seen it happen many times.

Prayer and action

It is a tragedy that anyone should regard prayer meetings as boring. Sadly, this often used to be the case for us, when we had a deadly sense of going through a routine that seemed unrelated to life. When we look at the prayer meetings in the book of Acts we always find them taking place against a background of action.

The events of Pentecost started with a prayer meeting, but they are so tied up with action that it is impossible to discern when the disciples ceased sitting in the house, in prayer, and began going out into the streets with power. The next recorded prayer meeting is preceded by a brief visit to jail; it concludes in a shaking building, crowded with people who have had a fresh instilling of the Holy Spirit.

After that, we find the church gathered at Mary's home because Peter is in prison again. The meeting was concluded not with a formal benediction but by the release of Peter, who actually found it more difficult to get into the prayer meeting than to get out of prison!

Another prayer group in Antioch witnessed the call and commissioning of Paul and Barnabas to their apostolic work. Prayer meetings were continually alive with the interventions of God.

Our times of church prayer should be part of a corporate lifestyle based on prophetic vision. If our local church is inactive and merely carrying out a routine, the prayer meeting will reflect that in lack of purpose and life. But if we are a people moving forward in God's purpose, our prayer times will be relevant and exciting. Evangelistic endeavor, special outreach, a need for a miraculous endowment of money, or some other goal will motivate us. Jesus said, "Ask that you may receive, that your joy may be full."

The boredom associated with prayer meetings in the past has often been caused by their predictability and lack of vital purpose: there was a Thursday night prayer meeting every week, whether or not anything special was happening. Eventually, people just "went through the motions."

Out of the rut

New Testament prayer meetings seem more spontaneous and related to life. Today, in the West, our church bulletins rarely include reference to the pastor's recent imprisonment for preaching in the open air. But even if circumstances do not demand emergency prayer meetings, we can still change things around from time to time.

We have experimented with weeks of non-stop church prayer, with people signing up for selected hours through a seven-day chain of day and night intercession. The numbers present for each hour varied from one or two to a dozen or more, but there was a great sense of church unity as one took over the baton from another. The church has kept a diary of any significant leading from the Holy Spirit and of subjects that were especially prayed over during each hour.

We have also divided a month between church house groups for days of prayer and fasting.We appointed groups to a day each, excluding weekends, to maintain the chain. After a day of fasting, the groups gathered on their specified evening to pray. As the month passed the whole church was drawn into the prayer battle.

More and more churches are feeling the call to corporate prayer. Some now have regular monthly church intercession times, others bimonthly. The meetings may well become increasingly frequent; there is no competition, but God is spurring us on in corporate prayer.

We need revival

There are more lessons to be learned, but let us be sure of this: revival is always preceded by strong corporate prayer, and, indeed, has often broken out in the very prayer meetings themselves. We must keep adjusting our programs in response to the leading of the Holy Spirit, and must have growing expectation for a genuine visitation of God. I thank God for the restoration we are enjoying today, but it is by no means the revival we so desperately need. God has not yet poured out the floods on the dry ground that our forefathers saw. The Puritans believed that

> the kingdom of Christ would spread and triumph through the powerful operations of the Holy Spirit poured out upon the church in revivals. Such periods would come at the command of Christ, for new Pentecosts would show him still to be both Lord and Christ.[2]

We still pray for the outpouring of the Holy Spirit, but how will this latter rain fall? Prophetic vision gets us moving in prayer, but how do we proceed in the midst of the coming blessing?

Ask for rain

Zechariah tells us to ask for rain in the time of the spring rain (Zech. 10:1). This chapter in Zechariah may at first glance appear obscure, full of mysterious allusions and figurative language; but closer inspection reveals that it is, in fact, describing an era much like our own. People are wandering about, prey to lies and deception, unshepherded, unguarded, vulnerable to false prophets and to those who claim supernatural powers.

God is angered, says the prophet, by those who are supposed to be leading but are not doing a proper job. When this failure occurs, the vacuum in leadership is quickly filled by those who lead poor, ignorant sheep astray. So what does the Lord do? He determines to punish the shepherds and visits the flock instead, as He did in Jesus' day!

The result of this visitation is that the poor, misguided flock is united and transformed into a "majestic warhorse"—a great vehicle of power and energy, a fearsome, awe-inspiring, effective tool of war. But not only is the flock to be thus transformed corporately, for individuals also will emerge with distinctive characteristics and function.

Key men

In telling of the work to be done in the time of the latter rain, Zechariah refers to the "cornerstone" (Zech. 10:4)—a key foundational stone, on which other stones are built: strong enough in that corner position to hold together walls coming from different angles; strong enough to be leaned upon, to unite, to support.

Then comes "the tent peg," whose special feature is to bring stability to an otherwise insecure structure. A tent peg can take the knocks that drive it deeper into the ground, growing more established and secure with every blow. It is designed to take the strain and tug of the ropes that hold the tent down, preventing it from being blown and tossed around by every wind of doctrine.

Next is the "bow of battle," which sends arrows speeding out to be embedded deep in the hearts of men, bringing them to their knees.

Lastly, we read of "rulers," who with authority restrain hostile enemies.

As these individuals emerge, the sheep now become "mighty men," treading down the enemy in battle.

This hitherto obscure Old Testament passage now sounds strangely familiar, reminiscent of another more explicit chapter in the New Testament. We can find a parallel in Ephesians 4, where we discover not sheep led astray by counterfeit gifts, but the church united in one body and spirit, the recipient of the grace of God. This grace is expressed in gifts given by an ascended, victorious Lord.

The gifts are first the apostle, who could be likened to a cornerstone, as was Jesus himself—"the apostle of our faith," uniting Jew and Gentile, tax collector and Zealot. Then comes the prophet with his dogged endurance, surviving the battering of misrepresentation. He is vital to the establishing of the church and firmly bedding it down on clear ground. "Bow of battle" could describe the evangelist, whose words have the power to penetrate and change the hearts of unbelievers; and "rulers" could speak of shepherds who know how to use their rods to beat off wolves.

The work of these leaders is to produce mighty men who tread down the enemy. So we find in Ephesians 4 that the gifts of God to the church are for the equipping of the saints and for building them up together into "a mature man."

No wonder Zechariah entreats us to "ask rain from the Lord at the time of the spring rain." We have seen some rain falling on the church as the Holy Spirit has come upon many, bringing enlightenment and vigor to a once weak and scattered people. But we have yet to see the downpour that will bring about the growth of a mature church, secure and invincible. The Ephesians 4 gifts are vital to her development. Let us cry out to God to continue to give His gifts, and then we must let them function to bring harmony and release power in the church.

We have already considered the roles of the pastor, evangelist, and prophet. Now we must turn our attention to possibly the most controversial figure—the apostle.

CHAPTER 12

Apostles Today?

My sister had just been converted and was trying to convert me. During our conversation she said, "I'm not afraid of death anymore; I know I'm going to heaven." It was the most presumptuous thing I had ever heard. How could anyone know they were going to heaven? Later that evening I myself was born again and understood that salvation was all through the grace of God—His wonderful gift. I knew I had everlasting life.

Some sixteen years later I heard some of my friends discussing whether or not they were apostles. Again, I was quick to judge. What arrogance! Who did they think they were?

Now I have come to see that the call to salvation and the call to ministry both come by the grace of God. Paul received not only the grace of salvation but also the grace to be an apostle, though he was "the very least of all saints" (Eph. 3:8) and "not fit to be called an apostle" (1 Cor. 15:9).

Back to the Bible

My problem regarding conversion was solved by getting back to the Bible instead of walking in a maze of human logic based on previous experience. What does the natural mind know about salvation? Nothing at all. I had to submit to God's revelation in His word. So with the question of apostleship. Can we dispense with apostles today? We may arrive at a variety of conclusions if we simply pool our own ideas. If we yield to the Bible, however, we shall find the true answer.

What is an apostle? The Greek word for apostle has its root in the verb "to send," so that an apostle basically means "a sent one." Jesus repeatedly referred to himself as one, having been sent from the Father. Bishop Lightfoot tells us in his commentary on Galatians that the apostle is "not only the messenger but the delegate of the person who sends him. He is entrusted with a mission and has powers conferred upon him."[1]

Three classes

We can distinguish three classes of apostle in the New Testament. First of all there is Jesus, "the Apostle and High Priest of our confession" (Heb. 3:1). Next there are "the twelve." Some have felt that this is the end of the story, and that Paul was raised up by God to replace Judas. It is argued that we never hear of the hastily appointed Matthias again; but actually we never hear of many of the twelve again, and the Bible nowhere states that Paul was one of the twelve. He clearly distinguishes himself from them in 1 Corinthians 15:5-8. The twelve were "apostles of the Lamb" called by Jesus during His earthly ministry. The replacement for Judas had to be one who had accompanied them from the beginning.

It could almost be argued that Paul is in a category of his own as "one untimely born" (1 Cor. 15:8). He was certainly given an extraordinary amount of revelation to contribute to the Scriptures. He was, nevertheless, commissioned by the ascended Christ, and must therefore be regarded as generally belonging to the category referred to in Ephesians 4:8-11, where we read that "He ascended on high . . . and He gave some as apostles."

Special pleading might also be made for James, the brother of Jesus (Gal. 1:19), who emerged as a leading apostle, though he seems to have been an unbeliever during Jesus' earthly ministry. In the council at Jerusalem he seems to have obtained an even more influential place than Paul or even Peter (Acts 15:13-21). Barnabas is also called an apostle (Acts 14:14), and his apostleship was recognized by the church at the same time as Paul's. Paul also speaks of Andronicus and Junia as being "outstanding among the apostles, who also were in Christ before me" (Rom. 16:7).

Only twelve?

Many have argued that there were only twelve apostles, but as Bishop Lightfoot points out in his commentary on Galatians, "Neither the canonical scriptures nor the early Christian writings afford sufficient ground for any such limitations of the apostolate."[2] Others have accepted that Paul, Barnabas, and James were apostles, but still claim that the apostolic ministry is a thing of the past. Howard Snyder writes:

> Some have argued that apostles no longer exist today, but this conclusion runs counter to Biblical evidence . . . . Nothing in Paul's treatment of spiritual gifts suggests that he was describing a pattern for the early church only. Quite the opposite. For Paul, the church is a growing, grace-filled body, and apostles are a permanent part of that body's life.[3]

Many who have reluctantly conceded that the gift of tongues might still be with us have continued to dismiss it by saying it is only the least of the gifts. The apostolic gift, if it is for today, certainly cannot be similarly shrugged off. After Jesus ascended, He gave apostles, prophets, evangelists, and pastor/teachers to equip the saints until the church is brought to full maturity (Eph. 4:12-13). We must not miss the vital word "until." Few would argue that the church has reached its full stature, and if any of these grace gifts is missing we will not reach God's intended goal.

We have epistles; who needs apostles?

It has been suggested that apostles are no longer needed today because we have the Bible. The New Testament letters of the original apostles are enough. Any Bible teacher can expound these great truths.

Some of our greatest teachers have indeed expounded the epistles with extraordinary life and power. However, the tragic fact is that instead of producing a mature church, held together by joints of supply with each part working properly (Eph. 4:16), they have produced preaching centers with huge congregations that disintegrate when the gifted preacher is removed from the scene.

That does not mean we should despise great Bible teachers. Far from it! But what is our goal in building the church? Surely, that in the end we have a mature expression of the body of Christ. The saints are not only to know sound doctrine but are also to be equipped for works of service. They have to find their particular gifts and contributions to church life and should be encouraged to function in them. All the gifts of the ascended Christ are needed to reach this maturity.

The apostles of the early church did not fulfill only the role of writing the inspired New Testament. (Only a few of the apostles actually wrote our New Testament, helped by others such as Luke, who claimed no apostolic calling.) Just as in the Old Testament there were prophets who contributed nothing to Scripture, yet fulfilled a genuine prophetic ministry, so there were New Testament apostles who never gave us a line of Scripture, yet had a vital role to fulfill among the churches of their day.

Master builder

One of the distinctive features of the apostle is that he is a master builder and foundation layer (1 Cor. 3:10). Paul did not regard his apostleship as a position in the church hierarchy. He did not see himself at the top of a corporate pyramid; he was not a CEO in a complicated church superstructure.

Paul had a stewardship from God: he was to proclaim the unfathomable riches of Christ and bring people to an assured understanding of what it is to be in Christ and have Christ in them. This was the burden of apostolic doctrine. Paul did not wonder what he would preach from town to town; he had a body of doctrine to deliver. He knew when the saints had grasped it, and he knew when they had drifted from it. He could see the creeping death of legalism moving over one congregation and warned another against the subtle dangers of mystic Gnosticism. Modern churches still need the authoritative word that will set them free from legalism, super-spirituality, and other dangers.

Many an evangelical has thought liberalism to be the great enemy, not recognizing other, perhaps more subtle foes. Legalism, for instance, can look like commendable zeal; but Paul had no hesitation in calling it another gospel, not to be received even from an angel. How many in the average evangelical church are deeply assured that they have been delivered from sin, have died to the law, and are free from all condemnation? Apostolic doctrine handled with apostolic authority and insight is desperately needed.

Often we are blind to our own faults or shortcomings. Sometimes wrong emphases can enter in, hardly noticed by a local church focusing on itself. Spiritual coldness, doctrinal off-centeredness, or incorrect practice can unobtrusively become part of a church's life.

One of God's great provisions to safeguard his church from going astray is a continuing apostolic ministry. The apostle, essentially a traveling man, is able to bring objectivity to his appraisal of a local church's condition. For instance, although the church in Thessalonica was in many ways exemplary, Paul wrote the believers there that he longed to see them so he could supply what was lacking in their faith (1 Thess. 3:10). Others, such as the saints in Corinth, Galatia, and Colossae, had much for which to thank God in Paul's care of their churches.

Feeling the need

To illustrate further, if a local church, for instance, has not only received an attitude of legalism but has actually built some of its church structure around it, who has the authority to bring correction? The elders often feel trapped within the framework and long for an outside voice to authoritatively proclaim the way forward. Indeed, it is very often the elders who most feel the need for the apostolic ministry. At a recent ministers' conference I addressed it was acknowledged that, even if they could not yet see all the scriptural basis for apostolic ministry, the ministers personally felt the need for such a figure to arise to help them in their leadership of the congregation.

Traditional churches are feeling the pressures of new life. Charismatic gifts are emerging; a desire for freer worship is being expressed. How are the leaders to proceed? Many are facing such issues and do not know which way to turn. Conferences for like-minded pastors will not provide the full answer, nor will charismatic organizations. God's way is to give apostles and prophets. He has simply appointed men with different gifts to do different jobs.

Paul's authority was not derived from a special title or office. It was the fruit of two things: first, the grace of God in calling and equipping him with a particular gift as an apostle, and secondly, the working relationship he had with any particular church or individual. For example, Paul's fatherly relationship toward the churches in Corinth, Galatia, and Thessalonica is plain to see; he writes to the Corinthians, " . . . in Christ Jesus I became your father through the gospel" (1 Cor. 4:15). He rejoices in their lives and their love, and weeps over their failures and shortcomings. And as their father he lovingly and forthrightly claims spiritual authority among them.

When writing to the church at Rome, however, Paul's style was different. He felt free to communicate, but did not adopt the same approach he had used with other churches. He had not yet seen the Roman church face to face; they were not his "children in the Lord."

Eldership appointment

Paul's fatherly care for the church was also demonstrated in his concern that they have local leaders. The appointment of elders was an important aspect of his church building program. The Holy Spirit appointed elders, but they received public recognition through the laying on of hands by the apostles or their delegates.

Modern churches have often resorted to electing their leaders; but those elected into office can similarly be voted out of office, so the temptation to be a man-pleaser is considerable. Appointed by the congregation, such leaders are accountable to the congregation. When there is no anointing, democracy is probably the safest form of church government. But when God begins to give anointed leadership, democracy must make room for Him to have His way.

In the New Testament the whole matter was far more charismatic, in the word's truest sense. The Spirit-led appointment of elders was an important part of the apostles' foundation-laying ministry. Without the Holy Spirit's guidance, we resort to man-made structures with varying degrees of success, even leading to manifest disaster. In recent days some have even found it difficult to elect new leaders because differences of opinion in the congregation make the required majority hard to find. Where there is no acknowledgement of charismatic gifts of leadership we are bound to hit problems.

The wise master builder will not select elders of his own choice in an arbitrary way. He will observe the way in which men have earned the respect and love of the people and are displaying the fact that God Himself has appointed them. The laying on of hands then becomes an outward acknowledgement of what God has done by His Spirit. It is also a time of further impartation of spiritual grace for eldership.

Regions beyond

Another major aspect of the work of an apostle is breaking new ground with the gospel. Paul was always looking for virgin territory where new churches could be built. As he set sail he inspired existing churches with his outreaching vision.

Paul planned to see the church at Rome on his way to Spain and be helped on his way by them (Rom. 15:24); so the Roman church was drawn into the apostle's missionary thrust into Spain.

Members of Paul's team kept the churches informed of his movements, and kept him informed of the churches' progress. Young Timothies were caught up in the world vision and were trained in the apostolic team. They learned in living situations.

Just as local pastors reproduce after their kind at home, then, apostles reproduce after their kind while on their apostolic journeys. Soon Timothy or Titus could be sent with Paul's full blessing to do the job he himself would have done. Thus the work was multiplied.

As a result of their travels the apostles not only opened up new areas but brought a sense of unity to the work of God at large. Because of this unity, Paul was able, through his contacts, to bring not only spiritual help but also material help to churches in need. The poor in Jerusalem, for example, were helped by the churches Paul visited elsewhere. It is clear from the New Testament that God never intended local churches to be isolated. Through their relationships, with the unifying work of an apostle, they are caught up in an international fellowship and in the worldwide spreading of the gospel. People in local churches who have no larger vision are often tempted to become inward-looking and negative; but where there is global vision and the stimulus of news from other growing churches, there is a strong desire for expansion.

What do you want to build?

Can we do without apostles? The answer very much depends on what we are aiming to build. If we want simply to preserve the status quo, certainly we can cope without them. If we want a nice, cozy, charismatic house group or a safe institutional church enjoying a little renewal now and then, we can find some of our hopes fulfilled. But if we want to see the church come to the fullness of the stature of Christ, to a mature man, it is essential for all the gifted men mentioned in Ephesians 4 to have their full place in our church life.

How do apostles emerge? Like evangelists and prophets, they are brought out by the sovereign choice and anointing of God.

Thus there is no apostolic succession, nor is there any one training ground that produces all these leaders. Paul emerged from a background different from that of the other apostles, but needed the assurance that those he knew to be apostles before him recognized his calling and would extend the right hand of fellowship to him, which, in fact, they were happy to do (Gal. 2:9).

If the apostle is only to work on virgin soil where Christ has not been named, is there any room in the West for apostles today? Christ is certainly named throughout the Western nations, but we all know in what way many of the 90 percent outside our churches use that name.

Church planting

The fact remains that if we are to see the tide turn in the nations, we need to plant a great number of new churches: churches that are healthy, powerful communities built firmly on God's Word and relevant to modern society. Such new churches *are* being planted today, motivated and overseen by apostolic ministry. In addition, churches that have been in existence for many years often seek the aid of this ministry to help them through barriers they had found impossible to penetrate on their own.

Several Old Testament books describe the work of restoration that took place after the Babylonian captivity. As Paul said, "These things happened to them as an example, and they were written for our instruction, upon whom the ends of the ages have come" (1 Cor. 10:11). We can identify wholly with Ezra and Nehemiah in the rebuilding program, and also derive great encouragement from Haggai and Zechariah as we rebuild the ruins of church life. Like Ezra, we need to recover fully the place of the Scriptures; and like Nehemiah, we find that much rubbish needs to be removed. Great tenacity is called for to see the recovery work completed.

Not imposed authority

One part of the contemporary apostle's role is to bring the measuring-line to church life to see if it matches up with biblical standards. That is not to say he will arrive uninvited at any local church to declare his judgments. If the mighty apostle Paul was not automatically recognized by all as an apostle, and if his presence was regarded by some as unimpressive and contemptible, we can be sure that far lesser apostles would find it very difficult to impose their authority, or, indeed, to be recognized at all!

The modern apostle will be regarded by some as simply a brother or a preacher, while to others he functions as an apostle. That presents no problem; it is not unlike the attitude Christians might have toward local pastor/teachers from other churches in their area. The uninvited apostle cannot impose his authority in other churches; nor should it be his desire to do so. He will, however, happily respond to requests from church elders who reach out for his help.

The modern apostle makes no claims to infallibility, and surely our understanding is that only God's Word is infallible, not the actions of even New Testament apostles. Hence we see Paul having to correct Peter for his wrongful action in connection with the circumcision advocates (Gal. 2:11-14). Surely no modern apostle would seek to put himself above the apostle Peter. We can rejoice that we now have the completed Scriptures, not to replace spiritual gifts or the Ephesians 4 ministries, but as a means by which we may test them to be assured that they are of God.

Apostolic teams

Like Paul, the modern apostle will find he cannot work alone. As the work multiplies he will draw colleagues to his side. We have coined the phrase "apostolic team," but we must be careful not to suggest something official by that title. There is no such thing as "team status." Paul sometimes moved with some men, sometimes with others. They did not thereby claim a peculiar

position as "team member." The arrangement was purely func-
tional and very fluid.

In sending Timothy, Paul was confident that he would remind
them of "my ways which are in Christ, just as I teach everywhere
in every church" (1 Cor. 4:17). The men who traveled with Paul,
and who were sent to and from him, multiplied the ministry. Their
relationship with Paul provided a setting in which they no doubt
developed their own "ways in Christ"; they would keep a strong
dependence on Paul, but would also develop their own special
contribution.

Some men traveling with an apostle will be like Barnabas—
former local leaders who have proved their worth at a flourishing
home church that is now sufficiently secure to release them.
Others will be young men like Timothy, who not only commend
themselves to the apostle, but also have excellent relationships
with local elders, who sense the hand of God upon them and
release them gladly to the larger work.

Care for the churches

So we have a company of men who know that their prime calling
is no longer to one particular local work—though their roots are
there—but to the church at large. Whereas once they had the care
of a local flock, they begin to develop a care for the churches (2
Cor. 11:28).

Within the so-called "team" there will be embryonic apostles
like Timothy; there will also be men with other gifts—prophets
or evangelists, for instance—whose roles will differ, but who find
a "team" relationship truly helpful in keeping them from being
isolated and vulnerable.

It is important to see that prophets, evangelists, and pastor/
teachers have different ministries and therefore will not try to
bring to a local church what in the end only an apostle can bring.
There is a danger, when a man moves into a different area of
anointing, that he will be ineffective, resulting in frustration and
insecurity. For instance: When trying to represent the apostle, the
pastor who is not truly apostolic will tend to either hold back

where he should be decisive, or compensate for lack of anointing by undue legalism, which promotes a system instead of life. The prophet will excite activity but tend to breed insecurity when he is not joined to an apostle. The evangelist will gather many people but not build them together.

As a team of men bond with an apostle in love and mutual respect, they become a mighty force in the kingdom of God.

Paul's travels took him across national borders from country to country. Often he was separated for long periods of time from churches he had fathered. By modern means of communication and travel, the twentieth-century apostle and his colleagues can be in much closer contact with the churches they serve. By telephone we can reach around the world by dialing a few numbers; by highways we can travel miles for an evening's meeting; by jet plane we can circle the globe in a few hours; by printed books and audio and video cassettes we can speak when we are not even present.

There are no international barriers to apostolic ministry, and, in fact, at one time the company traveling with Paul was comprised of men from several nations (Acts 20:4). Apostolic ministry transcends nationalism and does not attempt to super-impose one nation's culture on another. Some traveling ministers will count it their joy to stimulate the development of emerging apostles and prophets in other nations, and then to step back to let them fulfill their calling, as Barnabas did with Paul. God will thus raise up Antioch churches all over the world—churches of far-reaching vision that release fresh apostolic and prophetic ministry.

But, you might ask, what sort of churches? Are you not in danger of simply producing *another* church? Are you, indeed, not simply another denomination? To quote J. B. Phillips (out of context): "What a terrible thought!" (Rom. 6:2).

CHAPTER 13

A New Denomination?

"What denomination are you?" is a common question in Christendom today, but one which would have left the earliest Christians bewildered. It is a concept totally untouched by the New Testament.

What does the word actually mean? It has two main uses. It can mean to give a name or number to any group of people or things, for example, coins or weight. Secondly, it has come to have particular application in naming a religious body or sect with its own clear identity and organizational structure within the Christian church.

It is important to distinguish these two uses. The first use seems to have been present in the New Testament. Followers of Jesus Christ had to be given a name. They were called by different titles from the outset: "followers of the way" seemed to be popular, as well as "the sect of the Nazarenes." In Antioch, Christ's followers became known as "Christians." But each of these names actually describes the same body of people. They were not titles of different groups within the body of Christ.

The modern concept of denominations is quite different. When people speak of, say, the Methodist church, they are referring to a definite group of Christians throughout the world committed to a particular pattern of doctrine and practice. So today we find Christendom divided into a number of such denominations, and many would regard the whole church as the sum of all the denominations. This is a sadly mistaken concept.

Universal or local

The Bible knows only two expressions of the church: first, the *universal church*, as described by Jesus when he said, "I will build my church, and the gates of hell shall not prevail against it" (Matt. 16:18 AV). This is the sum total of all believers throughout the world. Secondly, Jesus referred to the *local church* when He gave instructions on resolving difficult relationship problems (Matt. 18:17). These are the only two ways in which the church is referred to in the Bible—the worldwide church and the local church.

A denomination is neither one nor the other. It is too small to be one and too large to be the other. Though a denomination may have a worldwide organization, it does not constitute the whole church; it is too small. Yet it is manifestly more than a local church.

So today we have large international organizations which call themselves churches but which have no place in New Testament thinking. Moving on from there, we find that Christian unity is often considered to be related to the denominational framework. It is supposed that if two or more of these man-made structures can become organizationally one, we are moving toward unity. But such organizations do not appear in the New Testament, and their alliances have no biblical significance at all, so they cannot be seen as fulfilling Jesus' prayer that we might be one.

No divisions in the body

There is in the Bible no thought of churches gathering under one doctrinal emphasis, such as the "Church of Breaking Bread," or in one country, such as the "Church of France." There may well be churches in or throughout France, but not the Church of France (or England, or any other nation).

Also, it is unbiblical for one church to impose authority on another, or even to seek authority from another. The churches Paul planted did not "come under" Antioch or form a worldwide Antioch church. Each church was independent of any organization of churches, yet fellowship was maintained between churches by frequent visits of traveling apostles and prophets who safeguarded them from wandering into error, such as isolationism or indifference to the body of Christ worldwide. Some may have, therefore, come within Paul's sphere of authority, but were not thereby indirectly under the church at Antioch, since no local church had such authority.

It is very important that we untangle such things in our minds so that we safeguard the New Testament doctrine and build well for the future. The New Testament churches were independent but not isolationist. They did not belong to an organization, yet they felt part of the whole. Their unity was on the basis of a common doctrine and was fostered through the visits of traveling ministries.

Paul denomination?

If several churches saw Paul as their father, was there not the danger of developing a "Paul denomination"? Actually, the question never seemed to arise at all. Certainly within the church at Corinth there were those who had their favorite teachers, claiming to prefer either Paul, Peter, or Apollos, but that particular childishness earned a swift rebuke from Paul, and did not represent anything like the modern concept of denominationalism. To Paul and all the early Christians there was no question about it: there was only one church, one body, one Lord, one faith.

That is exactly the position for us to adopt today! There is only one church. It consists of all born-again believers throughout the world, and they are beloved and precious for Jesus' sake. Together we constitute the glorious bride of Christ.

Part of the whole

It was not acceptable for local churches to divide over doctrine or allegiance to a particular apostle. They were to consider themselves part of the whole. They were " . . . in Christ Jesus, saints by calling, with all who in every place call upon the name of our Lord Jesus Christ, their Lord and ours" (1 Cor. 1:2). The fact that Paul served particular churches did not cut them off from others, although Paul's style or approach may have differed from that of Peter or Barnabas. His relationship with the churches was personal, not institutional. When he told the Ephesian elders that they would "see his face no more" (Acts 20:38), he did not promise that headquarters would send a replacement. Paul did not build such a structure, nor do we want to today.

Those who hold dear the subjects handled in this book live in a constant tension. They know themselves to be part of the whole body of Christ and want to work out that commitment as part of their commitment to Christ. They are, however, convinced that God has led them to follow the principles covered here. The result is that they often find themselves outside the traditional evangelical camp, not by choice, but through faithfulness to their heartfelt convictions. Their goal is certainly not to establish a new denomination.

Paul, the former Pharisee with a background of total orthodoxy and hatred of heresy, knew the pain of being called a "ringleader of a sect" (Acts 24:5). How those words must have cut into his heart! He expressed his commitment to Christ by replying, "I admit to you, that according to the Way, which *they call a sect* [author's emphasis], I do serve the God of our fathers" (Acts 24:14).

When I was asked to address a meeting of ministers in London, they invited me to speak on the topic "Restoration Churches and the Whole Body of Christ." I declined the invitation, stating that I did not believe in "restoration churches" but in the restoration of the church. They graciously changed the title, and I was happy to accept their invitation.

But, in the end, what should local churches call themselves? In the New Testament it was very simple. Locality was the only thing that divided the New Testament church. There was the church at Colossae, or at Corinth, or the churches throughout Judea. Today we have names in order to function in a modern society. Forms have to be filled in, bank accounts have to be opened. We must call ourselves something.

I well remember once visiting a young man in prison. At the gates I had to give an officer some information. When he asked what my status was, I replied, "A minister of the church."

"Which church?" he inquired.

In my zeal I replied, "The church in Seaford."

"Which church?" he pressed.

"The Christian church," I insisted.

"Oh, Christian *Science*," he concluded.

"No!" I finally conceded, "the Free Church."

"Oh, I see," he said, and filled in the form. The word "Free" answered everything!

Some have tried to avoid offense by sidestepping the word "church" and calling themselves "Christian Fellowship." "The church at Brighton" or the "the Brighton church," for example, sounds very offensive in other Christians' ears. It is difficult to be biblical without sounding presumptuous.

Many titles

The churches with which I work have a great variety of titles, I am glad to say. Some call themselves "New Covenant Church," others "Community Church," others "Christian Fellowship," another "New Life Church," and so on. At least the diversity challenges any thought of denominationalism. Each church understands clearly that it stands as an autonomous local work and is free to enjoy fellowship with other churches that I do not serve. I am glad that the churches have avoided names which emphasize any particular doctrine, though arguably the word "community" suggests some emphasis.

Denominationalism is at its worst when it is in one's spirit. If we, by God's grace and by obedience to His Word, can build according to New Testament doctrine, what we call ourselves will be quite secondary. Our priority will be a wholehearted desire to see the church of God in all its glory being manifested through local assemblies which, while honoring and respecting each other, remain free from the kind of organization that divides the body.

Peter tells us to honor all men. That means we must not dismiss those who are not "seeing our vision." We are to "love the brotherhood," that is, all who are our brothers in Christ. The Bible knows no other brotherhood. The more we come to value our own particular group the more we can be tempted to despise others in the body of Christ. We must beware of this (1 Pet. 2:17).

As apostles are raised up and ministerial teams multiply, it will be essential for good relationships to develop between them. The Ephesians 4 ministers have a significant part to play, not only in bringing the church to fullness of stature but also in bringing it into unity of faith.

Paul's plea for forbearance, patience, meekness, and humility provides the doorway into this unity. Surely it is only as we bow our heads and enter through that narrow way that we shall ever come to the glories that Ephesians 4 promises us. May God keep us humbly following our meek and lowly King as He inherits the earth.

CHAPTER 14

Upside Down Kingdom

Whn Jesus entered Jerusalem on a young donkey, He hardly appeared to fulfill the promise of the mighty King who had long been awaited by the Jews of His day. He came meek and lowly, and established a kingdom unlike any the world has ever seen.

The only time Jesus particularly pointed out to His disciples that He was their Master and Lord was as He disrobed, took a towel, and, as a servant, washed their feet (John 13:14). He did this as an example—a sort of visual aid. It would be inscribed forever on their memories. Many years later Peter was writing to elders, reminding them to be examples and not to lord it over the flock. "Clothe yourselves with humility," he continued, doubtless reflecting on that unforgettable night (1 Pet. 5:1-5).

Jesus is building His church and bringing in a kingdom, the very ethos of which was displayed in that amazing scene. He contrasted His kingdom with the world when He said: "You know that the rulers of the Gentiles lord it over them, and their great men exercise authority over them. It is not so among you, but whoever wishes to become great among you shall be your servant" (Matt. 20:25-26).

An enigma

Spiritual authority is an enigma. Jesus, their Master and Lord, washed the disciples' feet. He expected loyal obedience, but He was among them as one not to be served but to serve and lay down His life for the sheep.

The restoration of spiritual authority opens a way fraught with dangers. How easy to take hold of verses and drive them into false conclusions. How easy to lust for positions of prestige and power where authority can be exercised. How easy to totally miss the spirit of Christ!

At the beginning of the charismatic movement some expressed great fears regarding the resurgence of the gift of tongues; but, as David Lillie helpfully argues in that connection,

> It would indeed be foolish to disregard or deny the risk of satanic intrusion, especially into those spheres where the Spirit of God is manifestly at work. . . . Of course these things are dangerous—are they not the weapons of our warfare? The soldier in training must be taught to handle lethal weapons, and this is dangerous work. To opt out of the realm of the supernatural because of the risk of satanic deception amounts to an admission of defeat.[1]

Such wise counsel also applies in the sphere of spiritual authority. There are dangers, and no doubt there have been abuses, but this must not drive us away from God-given principles. Leaders must have freedom to lead, or we will never advance. Close inspection reveals what style leadership should adopt: Paul was like a "nursing mother" with the church at Thessalonica; they had become "very dear" to him (1 Thess. 2:7-8).

Beloved brothers

Paul wrote to the Philippians not as to underlings but to "my brothers, you whom I love and long for, my joy and crown," and he went on to exhort them to let their gentleness be evident to all (Phil. 4:1, 5; NIV).

Even when writing to the troublesome Corinthians, Paul's style is to exhort them in the name of Jesus (1 Cor. 1:10). He counsels them to see him not as their fearsome overlord, but rather says, "Let a man regard us in this manner, as servants of Christ and stewards of the mysteries of God" (1 Cor. 4:1).

When trying to establish his relationship with them Paul does not argue that God has set apostles first; he says, rather, "God has exhibited us apostles last of all" (1 Cor. 4:9). Later, in an objective teaching passage in the same letter, he reverses the order (1 Cor. 12:28), but not while handling relationship issues. Here he is quick to point out that even if he was writing apparently harsh words, "I do not write these things to shame you, but to admonish you as my beloved children" (1 Cor. 4:14).

Paul goes on to mention that he has a rod, but how reluctant he is to use it! "Shall I come to you with a rod or with love and a spirit of gentleness?" (1 Cor. 4:21). Elsewhere he says of the authority he undoubtedly has, "the Lord gave [it] for building you up and not for destroying you" (2 Cor. 10:8).

Winning the weak

Paul does not bully the weak into submission but tries a totally different tactic. "To the weak I became weak, that I might win the weak" (1 Cor. 9:22). He does not enforce his views but honors the dignity of his readers and their individual responsibility by saying, "I speak as to wise men; *you judge* what I say" (1 Cor. 10:15, italics mine). Nobody is trodden down by the mighty apostle's feet. Rather, he is happy to appeal to them "by the meekness and gentleness of Christ" (2 Cor. 10:1). So the spirit of Christ pervades the church.

Even those caught in sin are to be restored by the spiritual "in a spirit of gentleness" (Gal. 6:1), and the very opponents of the servants of God are not to be slapped into line. Timothy is told to "be kind to all. . . . with gentleness correcting those who are in opposition" (2 Tim. 2:24-25).

But was Paul always tender and gentle? What about the letter to the Galatians, where he prescribes a curse for even an angel who preaches another gospel (Gal. 1:8)? How firm he was with

Peter when he witnessed the latter's hypocrisy through fear of the circumcision advocates (Gal. 2:11-14). "You foolish Galatians, who has bewitched you?" he continues (Gal. 3:1). It would appear that Paul uses his authority more in connection with doctrinal matters than with pastoral concerns. Even here, though, he asks, "Have I therefore become your enemy by telling you the truth?" (Gal. 4:16). His pastoral heart always shines through.

To the Corinthians he confides: "For to this end also I wrote that I might put you to the test, whether you are obedient in all things" (2 Cor. 2:9), but sometimes he looked for acts of obedience that displayed a right attitude on their part.

Be imitators

Paul's main teaching style seems to have been to use himself as an example. "Be imitators of me, just as I also am of Christ" (1 Cor. 11:1). He constantly reminded the people about the kind of man he proved to be among them (1 Thess. 1:5).

Timothy's youth and timid style might have undermined his ministry. Having said, "Let no one look down on your youthfulness," Paul could have added, "Let them know who's boss—establish your authority!" Instead, he takes a different line: "But rather in speech, conduct, love, faith and purity, show yourself an example . . . " (1 Tim. 4:12; cf. Titus 2:7).

Paul further instructs Timothy not to "sharply rebuke" an older man but rather to "appeal to him as a father" (1 Tim. 5:1). However, those who continue in sin he is to "rebuke in the presence of all, so that the rest also may be fearful of sinning" (1 Tim. 5:20). He tells Titus to "reject a factious man after a first and second warning" (Titus 3:10).

I wonder when we last saw someone "rebuked in the presence of all" or rejected as factious after two warnings. Against the backdrop of love and grace and every effort to win people, Paul saw the need to use spiritual authority to correct and admonish. Why should we see it differently? "Because of the dangers!" you may answer. But so many Bible doctrines are dangerous.

Justification by faith could turn us all into antinomians; the sovereignty of God could make us all careless about the lost; the doctrine of the second coming can lead men to be extremists and to be work-shy. Many aspects of the gospel are vulnerable to misrepresentation. Shall we, therefore, abandon every doctrine capable of misuse? Of course not! The answer to misuse is, as we all know, proper use.

The Bible clearly shows us the way. Its essential spirit is one of love, patience, gentleness, and forbearance. Love is set before us as the ultimate goal (1 Cor. 13). I was deeply thrilled when a recent visitor to our church commented to his sister, "You're very much loved here, aren't you?" There are many observations he could have made on what had been a very full evening program, but this was his comment. Paul said that the goal of all his instruction was love (1 Tim.1:5). We might be weak in other areas, but if we come short in love we have missed the goal. The use of spiritual authority does not imply the abandonment of love; rather, as every parent knows, when properly used it displays another aspect of love.

The meek inherit

It is the meek who inherit the earth along with their meek and lowly King. The world does not believe this. They believe that the strong inherit through force and manipulation. They do not know the greatest truth in the universe: that One who humbled Himself to die on a cross has thereby obtained the position of highest authority. The world does not know that he who humbles himself shall be exalted. They have been lied to, but Christ brought the truth to us.

Jesus has inaugurated an upside down kingdom that will never pass away. It is breaking in on planet Earth now. The early church began preaching this "gospel of the kingdom" with amazing impact, knowing it must be preached to the whole earth before the end comes (Matt. 24:14).

Their contemporaries, alarmed, described the disciples as "the men who have turned the world upside down" and went on to add, "[they] have now come here" (Acts 17:6, Phillips). They were tending to come everywhere! Paul could say "in the power of the Spirit . . . from Jerusalem and round about as far as Illyricum I have fully preached the gospel of Christ" (Rom.15:19).

Whole cities turned out to hear the apostles; multitudes came into the faith, embracing its "upside down" values. The kingdom of God was no static concept but a mighty, living force in the earth.

As "upside down" standards grip the church we must go and proclaim them to our muddled society. As Eddie Gibbs says:

For Jesus, the kingdom of God represented a new order of things. This new order was no distant hope but already operative . . . .God's final saving act was already operative in Israel; now is the new creation, time of the new wine and the new cloak (Mark 2:21f.)! . . . His amazing words and miraculous deeds were signs of the coming kingdom. As his disciples were identified with him in his ministry and experienced the healing powers of the new age operating through them, so they became partakers of the kingdom. Wherever they went represented a frontier of the kingdom (Luke 10).[2]

Kingdom proclamation

An ignorant world, gripped by the power of the enemy, needs exposure not only to powerful preaching but also to a kingdom life that expresses God's new order of things. Thus His government increases (Isa. 9:7). The New Testament scholar Jeremias put it this way: "The kingdom does not stand still on a particular piece of ground—it is always in the process of being achieved."[3]

Those looking for restoration are not trying to build a small, inward-looking, "heavy-shepherding" movement with its adherents nervously submitted on every issue. They simply have a vision of a glorious church. God said to Haggai that He wanted

His house to be built for two reasons: He wanted to take pleasure in it and He wanted to appear there in His glory (Hag. 1:8). Now *we* are God's house (Heb. 3:6).

The outpouring of the Holy Spirit that began in the early sixties is now circling the globe. In some places traditionalism has already dampened its early fires. But where churches honestly embrace New Testament principles, God's Spirit continues to move unquenched.

Some Christians see no hope for this age short of the return of Christ. They focus on scriptures concerning "things waxing worse and worse," iniquity abounding, and the love of many growing cold. The return of Christ is presented as our only hope. It is viewed as a gigantic rescue operation that will save us from final eclipse. This would mean that the church would have failed to accomplish what Christ commanded.

Final victory

Those looking for restoration have a different view. But they do not stand alone in this outlook, as the following testimonies bear witness.

> I may not live to see it. But the day will come when there will be a great Revival all over the whole earth. He has said: "I come to give you life, and that more abundantly." Go on and preach His Gospel, for He has it in His seven-sealed book that there will be a time of refreshing till all the ends of the earth shall see the salvation of God. See that you are doing your utmost to hasten on that kingdom. For whatever else is shipwrecked on the face of God's earth the kingdom of the Lord Jesus Christ is sure to come into harbor.[4]

William Jay (1869-1953) shared the same vision:

> We have many and express assurances in the scriptures which cannot be broken, of the general, the universal spread

and reign of Christianity, which are not yet accomplished. Nothing has yet taken place in the history of divine grace, wide enough in extent, durable enough in continuance, powerful enough in energy, blessed enough in enjoyment, magnificent enough in glory, to do anything like justice to these predictions and promises. Better days, therefore, are before us, notwithstanding the forebodings of many.

I certainly do not write as one who has achieved the goal. I am very aware that God is continually widening our horizons. This is not the time for digging in to defend recently taken land. We must press on! There is so much more for us: our experience of signs and wonders is very limited, and we have hardly started to work out the social implications of the gospel. Though we rejoice in what we are experiencing there is no room for complacency.

Nor is our goal only to recover New Testament Christianity. The gospels, Acts, and the epistles reveal many imperfections in the early church. The New Testament itself encourages us to look forward to better days (Eph. 4:13). As Michael Griffiths has said:

> The New Testament does not teach the past perfection of the early church but rather points to a perfection of the church which is still to be achieved in the *future*.[5]

It is my great longing that Christians might look forward together—not glancing at one another with suspicion. God has chosen to display His infinite wisdom through imperfect creatures. We have this treasure in earthen vessels. Sometimes in contacting one another we are more conscious of the earthen vessel than the treasure! God sees us quite differently: He has accepted us in Christ and has clothed us with His beauty. We have one Father and are part of one body, redeemed by the same precious blood and destined for the same indescribable glory. Our differences as Christians shrink in comparison with the great truths that bind us together.

The fact remains that God is doing a great new work in the earth, affecting nation after nation. Amazing news reaches us from Korea, China, and other parts of the world. Our own team involvement regularly takes us to India, Africa, America, and Europe. On all sides a fresh wind is blowing. Where old structures impede the work of God, surely they must yield. In order to serve the purpose of God in our generation, we must see major changes in existing churches and plant many new churches that express the life of the Spirit.

May God help us to love and trust one other as we press on toward the twenty-first century, running a good race—our feet unencumbered by tradition, our eyes fixed on our eternal destiny, our ears awaiting our Master's welcome: "Well done, My good and faithful servant. Enter into the joy of your Lord."

NOTES

Chapter 3

1. Walter Chantry, *Today's Gospel* (Banner of Truth, 1970), p.55.

Chapter 5

1. W. Hacking, *Smith Wigglesworth Remembered* (Harrison House Inc., 1981), p.30.
2. D. Martyn Lloyd-Jones, *Joy Unspeakable* (Kingsway Publications, 1984), pp.16, 18.

Chapter 6

1. A.W. Tozer, *Worship: The Missing Jewel* (Christian Publications, 1961).
2. Tozer, *The Knowledge of the Holy* (STL, 1969; STL/Kingsway Publications, 1984).
3. C.H. Spurgeon, *Autobiography* (Banner of Truth, 1962).
4. D. Martyn Lloyd-Jones in *Westminster Record*, Vol. 43, No.9.

Chapter 7

1. E. Schweizer, article in *Interpretation*, xiii, 1959, p.401, quoted in Bruce Milne, *We Belong Together* (IVP), p.68.
2. John R.W. Stott, *One People* (Falcon Books, 1969).
3. Ibid.
4. Larry Christenson, *The Christian Family* (Fountain Trust, 1971; Kingsway Publications, 1981), p.79.
5. Ibid.

Chapter 8

1. John R.W. Stott, *The Preacher's Portrait* (Tyndale Press, 1961), pp.73,74.
2. Ibid.
3. *Brighton and Hove Gazette and Herald*, 11 Feb. 1984.

Chapter 9

1. Howard Snyder, "The Church as God's Agent in Evangelism," *Let the Earth Hear His Voice* (Copyright World Wide Publications: Minneapolis, 1975. All rights reserved. Used by permission.)
2. David Watson, *I Believe in Evangelism* (Hodder & Stoughton, 1976).

Chapter 11

1. Eileen Crossman, *Mountain Rain* (OMF Books, 1982), pp.127-128.
2. Iain Murray, *The Puritan Hope* (Banner of Truth, 1971), p.51.

Chapter 12

1. J.B. Lightfoot, *St. Paul's Epistle to the Galatians* (Macmillan & Co., 1981), p.94.
2. Ibid.
3. Howard A. Snyder, *Community of the King* (Copyright Inter-Varsity Christian Fellowship of the U.S.A., 1977). Used by permission of InterVarsity Press.

Chapter 14

1. David Lillie, *Tongues Under Fire* (Fountain Trust, 1966), p.44.
2. Eddie Gibbs, *I Believe in Church Growth* (Hodder & Stoughton, 1981), pp.63,64.
3. Joachim Jeremias, *New Testament Theology* (SCM Press, 1971), p.98.
4. G.F. Barbour, *Life of Alexander Whyte* (Hodder & Stoughton, 1923).
5. Dr. Michael C. Griffiths, "Unity—of the Spirit and of the Faith," C.R. Batten Lecture, 1984, given to the London Baptist Preachers' Association.

Also from Cityhill...

Is There Not A Cause?

Beyond the Disappointment of Aimless Christianity

By Joseph Tosini

Have you been promised miracle healing and financial prosperity only to discover that someone's faith-formula failed you? Do you still battle with problems from which you were supposedly delivered? Did you believe the predictions that Jesus would come back . . . in 1972 . . . in 1975 . . . in 1988? The repeated failures of contemporary Christianity raise disturbing questions. Can the church work? Can believers really live out the radical message of the Bible?

These were the questions Joe Tosini began asking years ago. He didn't retreat to a theological ivory tower. He simply gathered a band of zealous young believers who weren't afraid to upend some of the sacred cows of contemporary Christian practice. They sought to weed out religiosity and sidestep trendy teachings of Me-centered Christianity.

This book deals with serious issues, but along the way you'll meet a few fascinating characters. Like Henry, a near-sighted fructarian who stomped on his glasses in a fit of faith—only to find he couldn't see to drive.

Parts of this story can entertain you. But its main purpose is to instill hope. Hope that the church, despite its failures, can work. And hope that the years you invest in the central cause of Christianity will not be wasted.

Available in hardback from your local Christian bookstore or by sending $14.95 plus $1 for shipping to:

Cityhill Publishing
4600 Christian Fellowship Road
Columbia, MO 65201

Also from Cityhill...

Called Out

A Quarterly Journal Devoted to Building the Local Church

It doesn't take a Ph.D. to see that the church has shortcomings. Newspaper editors know it. Schoolteachers know it. Pastors know it. Everybody knows it.

So, is it time to draft the church's obituary? We don't think so. God has not given up on the church. Despite the soft spots, the church always was and always will be the key to God's eternal purpose.

We at *Called Out* want to contribute whatever we can to help build the church—not an anemic institution, but a courageous company determined to turn every community right side up.

Write today for a sample subscription: the next two issues of *Called Out* free of charge.

Send your request to:
Cityhill Publishing
4600 Christian Fellowship Road
Columbia, MO 65203